ROWAN

purelife

12 designs by Marie Wallin
in Rowan Purelife

**Organic Wool - naturally dyed**

**purelife?** this **eco-responsible** organic wool yarn keeps nature pure and life good for the farmers who make their living from the earth

**why organic wool?** our organic wool is grown in an environmentally and socially responsible way from sheep grazed on land free from pesticides and chemical fertilisers - our organic wool yarn conforms to the eu regulation 2092/91 for organic farming practices

**low impact dyeing?** our organic wool is cleaned and processed in an environmentally friendly way and then dyed with **natural sustainable plant dyes** producing no toxic effluent

**chicory** pattern page 42

**tarragon** pattern page 38

**thyme** pattern page 54

**bergamot** pattern page 36

melissa pattern page 56

chervil pattern page 49

**corriander** pattern page 40

## The Yarn

Our organically grown naturally dyed yarn knits to
standard DK tension. The yarn is coloured with plant
dyes and due to their organic nature some shade
variation will simply add to the yarn's unique
inherent beauty. To ensure the longevity of the yarn,
avoid prolonged exposure to direct sunlight and
follow the recommended wash care instructions found
on the ball band. These natural variations do not in any
way affect the quality or efficiency of the yarn.

# The Colours

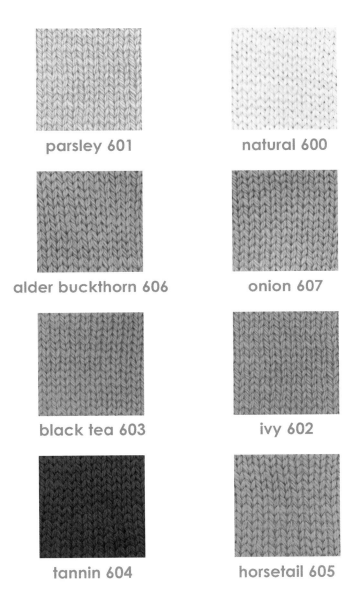

parsley 601

natural 600

alder buckthorn 606

onion 607

black tea 603

ivy 602

tannin 604

horsetail 605

# The Dyes

### Alder Buckthorn (Rhamnus Frangula)
The Alder Buckthorn is a slender shrub, widely distributed over Europe and Northern Asia. It is found in woods and thickets throughout England, although quite rare in Scotland. The bark and leaves of the Alder Buckthorn yield a yellow dye much used in Russia. The berries, when unripe afford a green colour, readily taken by woollen yarn; when ripe they give various shades of blue and grey. The medicinal properties of Alder Buckthorn include use as an intestinal tonic and laxative. It was also used as a very effective treatment against piles.

### Horsetail (Equisetum arvense, Equisetum hyemale, Equisetum maximum)
The Horsetails belong to a class of plants, the Equisetaceae, that has no direct affinity with any other group of British plants. They are nearest allied to the Ferns and their Latin name is derived from the peculiar bristly appearance of the jointed stems of the plants, which have also earned them their popular names of Horsetail, ottle-brush and Paddock-pipes. Medicinally in the past it has been proved useful in the treatment of consumption and dysentry.

### Onion (Allium cepa)
The onion is commonly grown and widely used as a vegetable. The onion skin has a long history of being used as a dyestuff to colour many different products. The onion skins are soaked and then boiled to extract the brownish colour. It has also been proved useful medicinally as an antiseptic and diuretic.

### Tannin
The name 'tannin' is derived from the French 'tanin' and is used for a range of natural polyphenols from animals, plants and minerals. In history the tanning of animal skins for protection was achieved with the use of plant tannins. Plant tannins used for dyestuffs are extracted from chestnut and oak wood.

### Ivy (Hedera Helix)

The plant is found over the greater part of Europe and northern and central Asia and is said to have been particularly abundant in Nyssa, the fabled home of Bacchus in his youth. It is well known as an evergreen, woody climber with dark green, glossy and angular leaves. The ivy plant produces berries and flowers at certain times of the year. It's use as a natural dyestuff is widely known with the leaves producing a yellow or green dye. Ivy gum or resin which is found on the stem has been used in the production of a red dye. The berries can also be used as a dyestuff. Unripe berries produce pinkish grey and greens, while the ripe berries produce a dull fawn colour. Ivy is now not known for it's medicinal properties, but in history it was widely used to prevent intoxication by wine.
Image - Forest & Kim Starr (USGS)

### Parsley (Carum petroselinum)

This widely grown garden herb is not indigenous to Britain. Thought to be a native plant of Sardinia, it was brought to England and first cultivated in the 16th century. Parsley was held in great esteem by the ancient Greeks, crowning victors at the Isthmian games and making wreaths for adorning the tombs of the dead. The herb was never used in cooking of old, being haled sacred to oblivion and to the dead. Parsley is widely used by the natural dyer by soaking and boiling the plant to extract it's soft stone colour. Medicinally the seeds are used for the extraction of an oil called Apiol, which is greatly used in the treatment of malarial disorders. Using parsley leaves to make tea proved useful in the WW1 trenches for the treatment of kidney complications when suffering from dysentry.

### Tea (Camellia thea)

A small evergreen shrub cultivated to a height of 7 to 8 feet, but growing wild up to 30 feet high and much branched. The leaves are used in the making of the popular drink. Black tea is produced by a lengthy process of drying and roasting. It is in this form that it is also used as a dyestuff, which is soaked and boiled in water to release the colour.

# Sizing Guide

When you knit and wear a Rowan design we want you to look and feel fabulous. This all starts with the size and fit of the design you choose. To help you to achieve a great knitting experience we have looked at the sizing of our womens and menswear patterns. This has resulted in the introduction of our new sizing guide which includes the following exciting features:

Our sizing now conforms to standard clothing sizes. Therefore if you buy a standard size 12 in clothing, then our size 12 or Medium patterns will fit you perfectly.

We have extended the size range of our patterns, with over half of the designs shown being available to knit from size 8 to 22, or Small through to Xlarge.

The menswear designs are now available to knit in menswear sizes Small through to XXlarge ie. 40" to 48" chest.

Dimensions in the charts below are body measurements, not garment dimensions, therefore please refer to the measuring guide to help you to determine which is the best size for you to knit.

## CASUAL SIZING GUIDE FOR WOMEN

As there are some designs that are intended to fit more generously, we have introduced our casual sizing guide. The designs that fall into this group can be recognised by the size range: Small, Medium, Large & Xlarge. Each of these sizes cover two sizes from the standard sizing guide, ie. Size S will fit sizes 8/10, size M will fit sizes 12/14 and so on.

The sizing within this chart is also based on the larger size within the range, ie. M will be based on size 14.

| UK SIZE<br>DUAL SIZE | S<br>8/10 | M<br>12/14 | L<br>16/18 | XL<br>20/22 | |
|---|---|---|---|---|---|
| To fit bust | 32 – 34 | 36 – 38 | 40 – 42 | 44 – 46 | inches |
| | 82 – 87 | 92 - 97 | 102 – 107 | 112 – 117 | cm |
| To fit waist | 24 – 26 | 28 – 30 | 32 – 34 | 36 – 38 | inches |
| | 61 – 66 | 71 – 76 | 81 – 86 | 91 – 96 | cm |
| To fit hips | 34 – 36 | 38 – 40 | 42 – 44 | 46 – 48 | inches |
| | 87 – 92 | 97 – 102 | 107 – 112 | 117 – 122 | cm |

## STANDARD SIZING GUIDE FOR WOMEN

| UK SIZE | 8 | 10 | 12 | 14 | 16 | 18 | 20 | 22 | |
|---|---|---|---|---|---|---|---|---|---|
| USA Size | 6 | 8 | 10 | 12 | 14 | 16 | 18 | 20 | |
| EUR Size | 34 | 36 | 38 | 40 | 42 | 44 | 46 | 48 | |
| To fit bust | 32 | 34 | 36 | 38 | 40 | 42 | 44 | 46 | inches |
| | 82 | 87 | 92 | 97 | 102 | 107 | 112 | 117 | cm |
| To fit waist | 24 | 26 | 28 | 30 | 32 | 34 | 36 | 38 | inches |
| | 61 | 66 | 71 | 76 | 81 | 86 | 91 | 96 | cm |
| To fit hips | 34 | 36 | 38 | 40 | 42 | 44 | 46 | 48 | inches |
| | 87 | 92 | 97 | 102 | 107 | 112 | 117 | 122 | cm |

## MEASURING GUIDE

For maximum comfort and to ensure the correct fit when choosing a size to knit, please follow the tips below when checking your size.

Measure yourself close to your body, over your underwear and don't pull the tape measure too tight!

**Bust/chest** – measure around the fullest part of the bust/chest and across the shoulder blades.

**Waist** – measure around the natural waistline, just above the hip bone.

**Hips** – measure around the fullest part of the bottom.
If you don't wish to measure yourself, note the size of a favourite jumper that you like the fit of. Our sizes are now comparable to the clothing sizes from the major high street retailers, so if your favourite jumper is a size Medium or size 12, then our casual size Medium and standard size 12 should be approximately the same fit.

To be extra sure, measure your favourite jumper and then compare these measurements with the Rowan size diagram given at the end of the individual instructions.

Finally, once you have decided which size is best for you, please ensure that you achieve the tension required for the design you wish to knit.

Remember if your tension is too loose, your garment will be bigger than the pattern size and you may use more yarn. If your tension is too tight, your garment could be smaller than the pattern size and you will have yarn left over.

Furthermore if your tension is incorrect, the handle of your fabric will be too stiff or floppy and will not fit properly. It really does make sense to check your tension before starting every project.

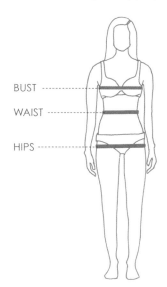

BUST

WAIST

HIPS

# The Gallery

**bergamot**
main image page 14
pattern page 36

**tarragon**
main image page 10
pattern page 38

**coriander**
main image page 22
pattern page 40

**chicory**
main image page 6
pattern page 42

**comfrey**
main image page 28
pattern page 44

**lovage**
main image page 4
pattern page 46

**marjoram**
main image page 26
pattern page 48

**chervil**
main image page 21
pattern page 49

**par-cel**
main image page 8
pattern page 50

**parsley**
main image page 24
pattern page 52

**thyme**
main image page 12
pattern page 54

**melissa**
main image page 19
pattern page 56

# Bergamot

main image page 16

## SIZE

|  | S | M | L | XL |  |
|---|---|---|---|---|---|
| To fit bust |  |  |  |  |  |
|  | 81-86 | 91-97 | 102-107 | 112-117 | cm |
|  | 32-34 | 36-38 | 40-42 | 44-46 | in |

## YARN

**Rowan Purelife Organic Wool DK**

| 14 | 14 | 15 | 15 | x50gm |
|---|---|---|---|---|

(photographed in Alder Buckthorn 606)

## CROCHET HOOK

4.00mm (no 8) (US G6) crochet hook

**BUTTONS** - 3 x 00411 toggle buttons

## TENSION

17 sts and 10 rows to 10 cm measured over tr fabric using 4.00mm (US G6) hook.

## UK CROCHET ABBREVIATIONS

**ch** = chain; **dc** = double crochet;
**dtr** = double treble; **ss** = slip stitch;
**sp(s)** = space(s); **tr** = treble;
**dtr5tog** = *(yoh) twice and insert hook as indicated, yoh and draw loop through, (yoh and draw through 2 loops) twice, rep from * 4 times more, yoh and draw through all 6 loops on hook;
**yoh** = yarn over hook.

**BODY** (worked in one piece to armholes)
Using 4.00mm (US G6) hook make 212 [236: 260: 284] ch.
**Row 1 (RS):** 5 dtr into 8th ch from hook, *miss 3 ch, 1 dtr into next ch**, miss 3 ch, 5 dtr into next ch, rep from * to end, ending last rep at **, turn. 26 [29: 32: 35] patt reps.
**Row 2:** 4 ch (counts as first dtr), 2 dtr into st at base of 4 ch, *miss 2 dtr, 1 dtr into next dtr, miss 2 dtr**, 5 dtr into next dtr, rep from * to end, ending last rep at **, 3 dtr into top of 4 ch at beg of previous row, turn.
**Row 3:** 4 ch (counts as first dtr), miss st at base of 4 ch and next 2 dtr, *5 dtr into next dtr, miss 2 dtr**, 1 dtr into next dtr, miss 2 dtr, rep from * to end, ending last rep at **, 1 dtr into top of 4 ch at beg of previous row, turn.
Last 2 rows form shell patt.
Work in shell patt for a further 8 rows.
Now work in bobble patt as folls:
**Row 12:** 6 ch (counts as 1 dtr and 2 ch), miss 3 dtr at end of last row, *dtr5tog into next dtr, 2 ch, miss 2 dtr, rep from * to last st, 1 dtr into top of 4 ch at beg of previous row, turn. 52 [58: 64: 70] patt reps.
**Row 13:** 4 ch (counts as first dtr), miss st at base of 4 ch, *dtr5tog into next ch sp**, 2 ch, miss 1 dtr5tog, rep from * to end, ending last rep at **, 1 ch, 1 dtr into 4th of 6 ch at beg of previous row, turn.
**Row 14:** 6 ch (counts as 1 dtr and 2 ch), miss (dtr at end of last row, 1 ch and 1 dtr5tog), *dtr5tog into next ch sp, 2 ch**, miss 1 dtr5tog, rep from * to end, ending last rep at **, miss last dtr5tog, 1 dtr into top of 4 ch at beg of previous row, turn.
Last 2 rows form bobble patt.
Work in bobble patt for a further 6 rows, ending after row 14.
**Row 21:** 3 ch (counts as first tr), miss st at base of 3 ch, 3 tr into each ch sp to end **and at same time** dec 6 [4:

2: 0] sts evenly across row by working 2 tr into 6 [4: 2: 0] ch sps evenly spaced across row, 1 tr into 4th of 6 ch at beg of previous row, turn. 152 [172: 192: 212] sts.
**Row 22:** 3 ch (counts as first tr), miss tr at base of 3 ch, 1 tr into each tr to end, working last tr into top of 3 ch at beg of previous row, turn.
Last row forms tr fabric.
Cont in tr fabric until body meas 34 [35: 36: 37] cm.
**Shape first front**
**Next row:** 3 ch (counts as first tr), miss tr at base of 3 ch, 1 tr into each of next 32 [36: 39: 43] tr and turn, leaving rem sts unworked.
Work on this set of 33 [37: 40: 44] sts only for first front.
**Next row:** 3 ch (does NOT count as st), miss tr at base of 3 ch - 1 st decreased, 1 tr into each tr to end, working last tr into top of 3 ch at beg of previous row, turn.
**Next row:** 3 ch (counts as first tr), miss tr at base of 3 ch, 1 tr into each tr to last 2 **tr**, tr2tog over last 2 tr - 1 st decreased, turn.
Working all decreases as set by last 2 rows, dec 1 st at armhole edge of next 3 [5: 6: 7] rows. 28 [30: 32: 35] sts.
Cont straight until armhole meas approx 13 [14: 14: 15] cm, ending at armhole edge.
**Shape neck**
**Next row:** 3 ch (counts as first tr), miss tr at base of 3 ch, 1 tr into each of next 17 [19: 21: 24] tr and turn, leaving rem sts unworked.
Dec 1 st at neck edge of next 4 [4: 5: 5] rows. 14 [16: 17: 20] sts.
Cont straight until armhole meas 20 [21: 22: 23] cm.
**Shape shoulder**
Fasten off.
**Shape back**
Return to last complete row worked, miss next 10 [12: 16: 18] tr, rejoin yarn to next tr, 3 ch (counts as first tr), miss tr at base of 3 ch, 1 tr into each of next 65 [73:

79: 87] tr and turn, leaving rem sts unworked.
Work on this set of 66 [74: 80: 88] sts only for back.
Working all decreases as set by first front, dec 1 st at each end of next 5 [7: 8: 9] rows. 56 [60: 64: 70] sts.
Cont straight until 2 rows less have been worked than on first front to shoulder fasten-off.
**Shape back neck**
**Next row:** 3 ch (counts as first tr), miss tr at base of 3 ch, 1 tr into each of next 14 [16: 17: 20] tr and turn, leaving rem sts unworked.
Dec 1 st at neck edge of next row. 14 [16: 17: 20] sts.
**Shape shoulder**
Fasten off.
Return to last complete row of back worked before shaping neck, miss centre 26 [26: 28: 28] tr, rejoin yarn to next tr, 3 ch (counts as first tr), miss tr at base of 3 ch, 1 tr into each tr to end, turn.
Dec 1 st at neck edge of next row. 14 [16: 17: 20] sts.
**Shape shoulder**
Fasten off.
**Shape second front**
Return to last complete row worked before shaping first front and back, miss next 10 [12: 16: 18] tr, rejoin yarn to next tr, 3 ch (counts as first tr), miss tr at base of 3 ch, 1 tr into each tr to end, turn. 33 [37: 40: 44] sts.
Complete second front to match first, reversing shaping.

## SLEEVES

Using 4.00mm (US G6) hook make 52 [52: 60: 60] ch.
Work rows 1 to 3 as given for body. 6 [6: 7: 7] patt reps.
**Row 4:** 4 ch (counts as first dtr), 4 dtr into st at base of 4 ch, *miss 2 dtr, 1 dtr into next dtr, miss 2 dtr**, 5 dtr into next dtr, rep from * to end, ending last rep at **, 5 dtr into top of 4 ch at beg of previous row, turn.
**Row 5:** 4 ch (counts as first dtr), 2 dtr into st at base of 4 ch, miss 1 dtr, *1 dtr into next dtr**, miss 2 dtr, 5 dtr into next dtr, miss 2 dtr, rep from * to end, ending last rep at **, miss 1 dtr, 3 dtr into top of 4 ch at beg of

previous row, turn. 7 [7: 8: 8] patt reps.
Work 3 rows.
Rep rows 4 and 5 again. 8 [8: 9: 9] patt reps.
Work 1 row.
Now work row 12 as given for body. 16 [16: 18: 18] patt reps.
**Row 13:** 5 ch (counts as 1 dtr and 1 ch), miss st at base of 4 ch, *dtr5tog into next ch sp**, 2 ch, miss 1 dtr5tog, rep from * to end, ending last rep at **, 1 ch, 1 dtr into 4th of 6 ch at beg of previous row, turn.
**Row 14:** 5 ch (counts as 1 dtr and 1 ch), miss st at base of 4 ch, dtr5tog into first 1-ch sp, *2 ch, miss 1 dtr5tog, dtr5tog into next 2-ch sp, rep from * until dtr5tog has been worked into last 1-ch sp, 1 ch, 1 dtr into 4th of 5 ch at beg of previous row, turn. 17 [17: 19: 19] patt reps.
Rep last row 2 [3: 4: 5] times more. 19 [20: 23: 24] patt reps.
Beg with patt row 14 as given for body, work in bobble patt for a further 3 rows, ending after row 14.
**Next row:** 3 ch (counts as first tr), miss st at base of 3 ch, 3 tr into each ch sp to end **and at same time** inc 3 [4: 1: 2] sts evenly across row by working 4 tr into 3 [4: 1: 2] ch sps evenly spaced across row, 1 tr into 4th of 6 ch at beg of previous row, turn.
62 [66: 72: 76] sts.
**Next row:** 3 ch (counts as first tr), miss tr at base of 3 ch, 1 tr into each tr to end, working last tr into top of 3 ch at beg of previous row, turn.
Last row forms tr fabric.
Cont in tr fabric until sleeve meas 40 [41: 42: 42] cm.
**Shape top**
Working all shaping in same way as for armholes and

front neck, dec 5 [6: 8: 9] sts at each end of next row. 52 [54: 56: 58] sts.
Dec 1 st at each end of next 9 [10: 11: 12] rows. 34 sts.
Fasten off.

MAKING UP
Press as described on the information page.
Join both shoulder seams using back stitch, or mattress stitch if preferred.
**Hem border**
With RS facing and using 4.00mm (US G6) hook, attach yarn at one end of foundation ch edge of body, 1 ch (does NOT count as st), work in dc evenly along entire foundation ch edge ensuring number of dc worked is a multiple of 6 sts plus 2 extra, turn.
**Next row (WS):** 1 ch (does NOT count as st), 1 dc into each dc to end, turn.
Rep last row twice more.
Place markers at both ends of last row.
**Next row:** 3 ch (counts as first tr), miss dc at base of 3 ch, 1 tr into next dc, *1 ch, miss 1 dc, 1 tr into each of next 2 dc, rep from * to end, turn.
**Next row:** 3 ch, miss 2 tr at end of previous row, *1 dc into next ch sp**, 3 ch, miss 2 tr, rep from * to end, ending last rep at **, 1 ch, 1 htr into top of 3 ch at beg of previous row, turn.
**Next row:** Miss first 1-ch sp, *5 tr into next 3-ch sp, 1 dc into next 3-ch sp, rep from * to end, replacing dc at end of last rep with ss into ch sp at beg of previous row.
Fasten off.

**Cuff borders (both alike)**

Work as given for hem border, working across foundation ch edge of sleeves.
**Collar**
Using 4.00mm (US G6) hook make 99 [99: 105: 105] ch.
**Row 1:** dtr5tog into 9th ch from hook, *2 ch, miss 2 ch, dtr5tog into next ch, rep from * to last 3 ch, 2 ch, miss 2 ch, 1 dtr into last ch, turn. 30 [30: 32: 32] patt reps.
Beg with row 13 as given for body, work in bobble patt until collar meas 10 cm.
Fasten off.
Easing in fullness and matching row-end edges, sew collar to neck edge.
**Left front band**
With RS facing and using 4.00mm (US G6) hook, attach yarn at top of collar, 1 ch (does NOT count as st), work in dc evenly down row-end edge of collar, then down row-end edge of left front to marker, turn.
**Next row (WS):** 1 ch (does NOT count as st), 1 dc into each dc to end, turn.
Rep last row twice more.
Fasten off.
Mark positions for 3 buttons along left front band - first to come 18 cm up from lower edge, last to come just below collar seam, and third evenly spaced between.
**Right front band**
Work to match left front band, making button loops in last row to correspond with positions marked for buttons by replacing (1 dc into each of next 2 dc) with (1 dc into next dc, 10 ch, 1 dc into next dc).
See information page for finishing instructions, setting in sleeves using the set-in method.

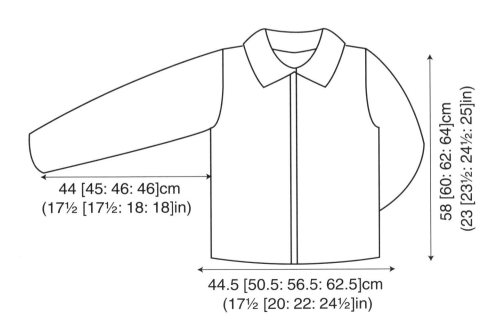

44 [45: 46: 46]cm
(17½ [17½: 18: 18]in)

44.5 [50.5: 56.5: 62.5]cm
(17½ [20: 22: 24½]in)

58 [60: 62: 64]cm
(23 [23½: 24½: 25]in)

# Tarragon
main image page 10

## SIZE

| 8 | 10 | 12 | 14 | 16 | 18 | 20 | 22 | |
|---|----|----|----|----|----|----|----|---|
| To fit bust | | | | | | | | |
| 81 | 86 | 91 | 97 | 102 | 107 | 112 | 117 | cm |
| 32 | 34 | 36 | 38 | 40 | 42 | 44 | 46 | in |

## YARN

**Rowan Purelife Organic Wool DK**

| 11 | 11 | 11 | 12 | 13 | 14 | 14 | 15 x50gm |
|----|----|----|----|----|----|----|----------|

(photographed in Ivy 602)

## NEEDLES

1 pair 3¾mm (no 9) (US 5) needles
1 pair 4mm (no 8) (US 6) needles
Cable needle

## BUTTONS – 5 x 00417

## TENSION

22 sts and 30 rows to 10 cm measured over st st
using 4mm (US 6) needles.

## SPECIAL ABBREVIATIONS

**C8B** = slip next 4 sts onto cable needle and leave
at back of work, K4, then K4 from cable needle.

## BACK

Using 3¾mm (US 5) needles cast on 165 [169: 173:
181: 187: 193: 201: 207] sts.
**Row 1 (RS):** K1, *P1, K1, rep from * to end.
**Row 2:** As row 1.
These 2 rows form moss st.
Work in moss st for a further 2 rows, ending with RS
facing for next row.
Change to 4mm (US 6) needles.
Now work in lower cable patt as folls:
**Row 1 (RS):** K21 [23: 25: 29: 32: 35: 39: 42], *moss
st 2 sts, K8, moss st 2 sts, K25, rep from * twice more,
moss st 2 sts, K8, moss st 2 sts, K to end.
**Row 2:** P21 [23: 25: 29: 32: 35: 39: 42], *moss st 2 sts,
P8, moss st 2 sts, P25, rep from * twice more, moss st
2 sts, P8, moss st 2 sts, P to end.
**Rows 3 to 6:** As rows 1 and 2, twice.
**Row 7:** K21 [23: 25: 29: 32: 35: 39: 42], *moss st 2 sts,
C8B, moss st 2 sts, K25, rep from * twice more, moss
st 2 sts, C8B, moss st 2 sts, K to end.
**Row 8:** As row 2.
**Rows 9 and 10:** As rows 1 and 2.
These 10 rows form lower cable patt.
Cont in patt, dec 1 st at each end of 7th [7th: 7th:
9th: 9th: 13th: 13th: 15th] and every foll 6th row
until 151 [155: 159: 167: 173: 179: 187: 193] sts
rem.
Cont straight until back meas 21 [21: 21: 22: 22: 24:
24: 26] cm, ending with RS facing for next row.
**Form pleats**
**Next row (RS):** K14 [16: 18: 22: 25: 28: 32: 35], *cast
off next 13 sts, K until there are 24 sts on right needle
after cast-off, rep from * twice more, cast off next 13 sts,
K to end. 99 [103: 107: 115: 121: 127: 135: 141] sts.
**Next row:** *P to within 1 st of next set of cast-off sts, P2tog
(these are sts either side of cast-off sts), rep from * 3 times
more, P to end. 95 [99: 103: 111: 117: 123: 131: 137] sts.
Now work in upper cable patt as folls:

**Row 1 (RS):** K7 [9: 11: 15: 18: 21: 25: 28], *K1, P1, K8,
P1, K12, rep from * twice more, K1, P1, K8, P1, K to end.
**Row 2:** P7 [9: 11: 15: 18: 21: 25: 28], *K1, P10, K1,
P11, rep from * twice more, K1, P10, K1, P to end.
**Rows 3 to 6:** As rows 1 and 2, twice.
**Row 7:** K7 [9: 11: 15: 18: 21: 25: 28], *K1, P1, C8B, P1,
K12, rep from * twice more, K1, P1, C8B, P1, K to end.
**Row 8:** As row 2.
**Rows 9 and 10:** As rows 1 and 2.
These 10 rows form upper cable patt.
Cont in patt, inc 1 st at each end of next and every foll
6th row until there are 109 [113: 117: 125: 131: 137:
145: 151] sts, taking inc sts into st st.
Cont straight until back meas 41 [41: 40: 43: 42: 44:
43: 45] cm, ending with RS facing for next row.
**Shape armholes**
Keeping patt correct, cast off 4 [5: 5: 6: 6: 7: 7: 8] sts at beg
of next 2 rows. 101 [103: 107: 113: 119: 123: 131: 135] sts.
Dec 1 st at each end of next 5 [5: 7: 7: 9: 9: 11: 11]
rows, then on foll 3 [3: 2: 3: 3: 3: 3: 4] alt rows.
85 [87: 89: 93: 95: 99: 103: 105] sts.
Cont straight until armhole meas 18 [18: 19: 19: 20: 20:
21: 21] cm, ending with RS facing for next row.
**Shape shoulders and back neck**
**Next row (RS):** Cast off 7 [7: 8: 8: 8: 9: 10: 10] sts, patt
until there are 20 [21: 21: 23: 23: 24: 25: 26] sts on
right needle and turn, leaving rem sts on a holder.
Work each side of neck separately.
Cast off 3 sts at beg of next row, 7 [7: 8: 8: 8: 9: 10] sts
at beg of foll row, then 3 sts at beg of next row.
Cast off rem 7 [8: 7: 9: 9: 9: 9: 10] sts.
With RS facing, rejoin yarn to rem sts, cast off centre
31 [31: 31: 31: 33: 33: 33: 33] sts, patt to end.
Complete to match first side, reversing shapings.

## LEFT FRONT

Using 3¾mm (US 5) needles cast on 86 [88: 90: 94: 97:
100: 104: 107] sts.

**Row 1 (RS):** *K1, P1, rep from * to last 0 [0: 0: 0: 1:
0: 0: 1] st, K0 [0: 0: 0: 1: 0: 0: 1].
**Row 2:** K0 [0: 0: 0: 1: 0: 0: 1], *P1, K1, rep from * to end.
These 2 rows form moss st.
Work in moss st for 1 more row, ending with **WS** facing
for next row.
**Row 4 (WS):** Moss st 5 sts and slip these 5 sts onto a
holder, M1, moss st to end.
82 [84: 86: 90: 93: 96: 100: 103] sts.
Change to 4mm (US 6) needles.
Now work in lower cable patt as folls:
**Row 1 (RS):** K21 [23: 25: 29: 32: 35: 39: 42], moss
2 sts, K8, moss st 2 sts, K25, moss st 2 sts, K8, moss
2 sts, K to end.
**Row 2:** P12, moss st 2 sts, P8, moss st 2 sts, P25, moss
st 2 sts, P8, moss st 2 sts, P to end.
**Rows 3 to 6:** As rows 1 and 2, twice.
**Row 7:** K21 [23: 25: 29: 32: 35: 39: 42], moss st 2 sts,
C8B, moss st 2 sts, K25, moss st 2 sts, C8B, moss st
2 sts, K to end.
**Row 8:** As row 2.
**Rows 9 and 10:** As rows 1 and 2.
These 10 rows form lower cable patt.
Cont in patt, dec 1 st at beg of 7th [7th: 7th: 9th: 9th:
13th: 13th: 15th] and every foll 6th row until 75 [77:
79: 83: 86: 89: 93: 96] sts rem.
Cont straight until left front meas 21 [21: 21: 22: 22:
24: 24: 26] cm, ending with RS facing for next row.
**Form pleats**
**Next row (RS):** K14 [16: 18: 22: 25: 28: 32: 35], cast
off next 13 sts, K until there are 24 sts on right needle
after cast-off, cast off next 13 sts, K to end.
49 [51: 53: 57: 60: 63: 67: 70] sts.
**Next row:** *P to within 1 st of next set of cast-off sts,
P2tog (these are sts either side of cast-off sts), rep from
* once more, P to end. 47 [49: 51: 55: 58: 61: 65: 68] sts.
Now work in upper cable patt as folls:
**Row 1 (RS):** K7 [9: 11: 15: 18: 21: 25: 28], K1, P1, K8,

P1, K13, P1, K8, P1, K to end.
**Row 2:** P5, K1, P10, K1, P11, K1, P10, K1, P to end.
**Rows 3 to 6:** As rows 1 and 2, twice.
**Row 7:** K7 [9: 11: 15: 18: 21: 25: 28], K1, P1, C8B, P1, K13, P1, C8B, P1, K to end.
**Row 8:** As row 2.
**Rows 9 and 10**: As rows 1 and 2.
These 10 rows form upper cable patt.
Cont in patt, inc 1 st at beg of next and every foll 6th row until there are 54 [56: 58: 62: 65: 68: 72: 75] sts, taking inc sts into st st.
Cont straight until left front matches back to beg of armhole shaping, ending with RS facing for next row.
**Shape armhole**
Keeping patt correct, cast off 4 [5: 5: 6: 6: 7: 7: 8] sts at beg of next row. 50 [51: 53: 56: 59: 61: 64: 67] sts.
Work 1 row.
Dec 1 st at armhole edge of next 5 [5: 7: 7: 9: 9: 10: 10] rows, then on foll 1 [1: 0: 0: 0: 0: 0: 0] alt rows. 44 [45: 46: 49: 50: 52: 55: 57] sts.
Work 1 [1: 1: 1: 1: 1: 0: 0] row, ending with RS facing for next row.
**Shape front slope**
Keeping patt correct, dec 1 st at end of next and foll 20 [20: 20: 20: 21: 21: 21: 21] alt rows **and at same time** dec 1 st at armhole edge of next and foll 1 [1: 1: 2: 2: 2: 3: 4] alt rows. 21 [22: 23: 25: 25: 27: 29: 30] sts.
Cont straight until left front matches back to beg of shoulder shaping, ending with RS facing for next row.
**Shape shoulder**
Cast off 7 [7: 8: 8: 8: 9: 10: 10] sts at beg of next and foll alt row.
Work 1 row.
Cast off rem 7 [8: 7: 9: 9: 9: 9: 10] sts.

**RIGHT FRONT**
Using 3¾mm (US 5) needles cast on 86 [88: 90: 94: 97: 100: 104: 107] sts.
**Row 1 (RS):** K0 [0: 0: 0: 1: 0: 0: 1], *P1, K1, rep from * to end.
**Row 2:** *K1, P1, rep from * to last 0 [0: 0: 0: 1: 0: 0: 1] st, K0 [0: 0: 0: 1: 0: 0: 1].
These 2 rows form moss st.
Work in moss st for 1 more row, ending with **WS** facing for next row.
**Row 4 (WS):** Moss st to last 5 sts, M1 and turn, leaving rem 5 sts on a holder. 82 [84: 86: 90: 93: 96: 100: 103] sts.
Change to 4mm (US 6) needles.
Now work in lower cable patt as folls:
**Row 1 (RS):** K12, moss st 2 sts, K8, moss st 2 sts, K25, moss st 2 sts, K8, moss st 2 sts, K to end.
**Row 2:** P21 [23: 25: 29: 32: 35: 39: 42], moss st 2 sts, P8, moss st 2 sts, P25, moss st 2 sts, P8, moss st 2 sts, P to end.
**Rows 3 to 6:** As rows 1 and 2, twice.
**Row 7:** K12, moss st 2 sts, C8B, moss st 2 sts, K25, moss st 2 sts, C8B, moss st 2 sts, K to end.
**Row 8:** As row 2.
**Rows 9 and 10:** As rows 1 and 2.
These 10 rows form lower cable patt.
Cont in patt, dec 1 st at end of 7th [7th: 7th: 9th: 9th: 13th: 13th: 15th] and every foll 6th row until 75 [77: 79: 83: 86: 89: 93: 96] sts rem.

Cont straight until right front meas 21 [21: 21: 22: 22: 24: 24: 26] cm, ending with RS facing for next row.
**Form pleats**
**Next row (RS):** K12, cast off next 13 sts, K until there are 24 sts on right needle after cast-off, cast off next 13 sts, K to end. 49 [51: 53: 57: 60: 63: 67: 70] sts.
**Next row:** *P to within 1 st of next set of cast-off sts, P2tog (these are sts either side of cast-off sts), rep from * once more, P to end. 47 [49: 51: 55: 58: 61: 65: 68] sts.
Now work in upper cable patt as folls:
**Row 1 (RS):** K6, P1, K8, P1, K13, P1, K8, P1, K to end.
**Row 2:** P7 [9: 11: 15: 18: 21: 25: 28], K1, P10, K1, P11, K1, P10, K1, P to end.
**Rows 3 to 6:** As rows 1 and 2, twice.
**Row 7:** K6, P1, C8B, P1, K13, P1, C8B, P1, K to end.
**Row 8:** As row 2.
**Rows 9 and 10:** As rows 1 and 2.
These 10 rows form upper cable patt.
Cont in patt, inc 1 st at end of next and every foll 6th row until there are 54 [56: 58: 62: 65: 68: 72: 75] sts, taking inc sts into st st.
Complete to match left front, reversing shapings.

**SLEEVES**
Using 3¾mm (US 5) needles cast on 45 [45: 47: 47: 49: 49: 51: 51] sts.
Work in moss st as given for back for 4 rows, ending with RS facing for next row.
Change to 4mm (US 6) needles.
Beg with a K row, work in st st, inc 1 st at each end of 3rd and every foll 6th [4th: 4th: 4th: 4th: 4th: 4th: 4th] row to 85 [53: 53: 59: 57: 63: 69: 75] sts, then on every foll - [6th: 6th: 6th: 6th: 6th: 6th: 6th] row until there are - [87: 89: 91: 93: 95: 97: 99] sts.
Cont straight until sleeve meas 44 [44: 45: 45: 46: 46: 45: 45] cm, ending with RS facing for next row.
**Shape top**
Cast off 4 [5: 5: 6: 6: 7: 7: 8] sts at beg of next 2 rows. 77 [77: 79: 79: 81: 81: 83: 83] sts.
Dec 1 st at each end of next 5 rows, then on every foll alt row to 55 sts, then on foll 9 rows, ending with RS facing for next row. 37 sts.
Cast off 4 sts at beg of next 4 rows.

Cast off rem 21 sts.
**MAKING UP**
Press as described on the information page.
Join both shoulder seams using back stitch, or mattress stitch if preferred.
**Left front band and collar**
Slip 5 sts from left front holder onto 3¾mm (US 5) needles and rejoin yarn with RS facing.
Cont in moss st as set until band, when slightly stretched, fits up left front opening edge to beg of front slope shaping, ending with RS facing for next row.
**Shape for collar**
Inc 1 st at beg of next and every foll alt row until there are 23 sts, taking inc sts into moss st.
Cont straight until collar section, unstretched, fits up left front slope to shoulder, ending at outer straight edge.
**Next row:** Moss st to last 4 sts, wrap next st (by slipping next st from left needle to right needle, taking yarn to opposite side of work between needles and then slipping same st back onto left needle - when working back across wrapped sts, work the wrapped loop and the wrapped st together) and turn.
Work 5 rows.
Rep last 6 rows until this section fits across to centre back neck.
Cast off in moss st.
Slip st band section in place. Mark positions for 5 buttons on this band - first to come 10 cm up from cast-on edge, last to come 2 cm below beg of front slope shaping and rem 3 buttons evenly spaced between.
**Right front band and collar**
Slip 5 sts from right front holder onto 3¾mm (US 5) needles and rejoin yarn with **WS** facing.
Work to match left front band and collar, reversing shaping and with the addition of 5 buttonholes worked to correspond with positions marked for buttons as folls:
**Buttonhole row (RS):** Moss st 1 st, work 2 tog, yrn (to make a buttonhole), moss st 2 sts.
Join cast-off edges of collar sections, then slip stitch right band and collars in place. On inside, form cast-off edges at waist level into pleats and and neatly stitch in place.
See information page for finishing instructions, setting in sleeves using the set-in method.

44 [44: 45: 45: 46: 46: 45: 45]cm
(17½ [17½: 17½: 17½: 18: 18: 17½: 17½]in)

61 [61: 61: 64: 64: 66: 66: 68]cm
(24 [24: 24: 25: 25: 26: 26: 27]in)

44 [46: 47.5: 51.5: 54: 57: 60.5: 63]cm
(17½ [18: 18½: 20½: 21½: 22½: 24: 25]in)

# Coriander

main image page 22

## SIZE

| | S | M | L | XL | |
|---|---|---|---|---|---|
| To fit bust | | | | | |
| | 81-86 | 91-97 | 102-107 | 112-117 | cm |
| | 32-34 | 36-38 | 40-42 | 44-46 | in |

## YARN

**Rowan Purelife Organic Wool DK**

| | | | | |
|---|---|---|---|---|
| 9 | 10 | 11 | 12 | x 50gm |

(photographed in Tanin 604)

## NEEDLES

1 pair 3¾mm (no 9) (US 5) needles

## TENSION

22 sts and 40 rows to 10 cm measured over patt using 3¾mm (US 5) needles.

## BACK

Using 3¾mm (US 5) needles cast on 107 [119: 133: 145] sts.
**Row 1 (RS):** Knit.
**Row 2:** K1 [3: 2: 0], P1, *K3, P1, rep from * to last 1 [3: 2: 0] sts, K1 [3: 2: 0].
**Rows 3 to 6:** As rows 1 and 2, twice.
**Row 7:** Knit.
**Row 8:** K3 [1: 0: 2], P1, *K3, P1, rep from * to last 3 [1: 0: 2] sts, K3 [1: 0: 2].
**Rows 9 to 12:** As rows 7 and 8, twice.
These 12 rows form patt.
Cont in patt until back meas 18 [19: 20: 22] cm, ending with RS facing for next row.
**Place belt openings**
**Next row (RS):** K11 and turn, leaving rem sts on a holder.
Work in patt on these 11 sts only for a further 14 rows, ending with **WS** facing for next row.
Break yarn and leave sts on a 2nd holder.
Return to sts left on first holder, rejoin yarn with RS facing and K to last 11 sts, turn and leave rem 11 sts on first holder.
Work in patt on these 85 [97: 111: 123] sts only for a further 14 rows, ending with **WS** facing for next row.
Break yarn and leave sts on a 3rd holder.
Return to sts left on first holder, rejoin yarn with RS facing and K to end.
Work in patt on these 11 sts only for a further 14 rows, ending with **WS** facing for next row.
**Join sections**
**Next row (WS):** Patt 11 sts of last section, then patt 85 [97: 111: 123] sts on 3rd holder, then patt 11 sts on 2nd holder. 107 [119: 133: 145] sts.
Work 28 [28: 28: 24] rows, ending with RS facing for next row. (Back should meas 29 [30: 31: 32] cm.)
**Shape for cap sleeves**
Inc 1 st at each end of next and 2 foll 8th rows, then on

2 foll 6th rows, then on 3 foll 4th rows, then on foll alt row, then on 2 foll rows, taking inc sts into patt and ending with **WS** facing for next row.
129 [141: 155: 167] sts.
Place markers at both ends of last row to denote base of armhole opening.
Cont straight until work meas 18 [19: 20: 21] cm from markers, ending with RS facing for next row.
**Shape shoulders and back neck**
**Next row (RS):** Cast off 10 [12: 13: 15] sts, K until there are 40 [44: 49: 53] sts on right needle and turn, leaving rem sts on a holder.
Work each side of neck separately.
Cast off 3 sts at beg of next row, and 11 [12: 13: 15] sts at beg of foll row.
Rep last 2 rows once more.
Cast off 3 sts at beg of next row.
Cast off rem 9 [11: 14: 14] sts.
With RS facing, rejoin yarn to rem sts, cast off centre 29 [29: 31: 31] sts, K to end.
Complete to match first side, reversing shapings.

## LEFT FRONT

Using 3¾mm (US 5) needles cast on 71 [77: 84: 90] sts.
**Row 1 (RS):** Knit.
**Row 2:** K1 [3: 2: 0], P1, *K3, P1, rep from * to last st, K1.
**Rows 3 to 6:** As rows 1 and 2, twice.
**Row 7:** Knit.
**Row 8:** K3 [1: 0: 2], P1, *K3, P1, rep from * to last 3 sts, K3.
**Rows 9 to 12:** As rows 7 and 8, twice.
These 12 rows form patt.
Cont in patt until left front meas 18 [19: 20: 22] cm, ending with RS facing for next row.
**Place belt opening**
**Next row (RS):** K11 and turn, leaving rem sts on a holder.

Work in patt on these 11 sts only for a further 14 rows, ending with **WS** facing for next row.
Break yarn and leave sts on a 2nd holder.
Return to sts left on first holder, rejoin yarn with RS facing and K to end.
Work in patt on these 60 [66: 73: 79] sts only for a further 14 rows, ending with **WS** facing for next row.
**Join sections**
**Next row (WS):** Patt 60 [66: 73: 79] sts of last section, then patt 11 sts on 2nd holder. 71 [77: 84: 90] sts.
**Shape front slope**
Keeping patt correct, dec 1 st at end of next and foll 13 [12: 12: 11] alt rows. 57 [64: 71: 78] sts.
Work 1 [3: 3: 1] rows, ending with RS facing for next row.
**Shape for cap sleeve**
Taking inc sts into patt, inc 1 st at beg of next and 2 foll 8th rows, then on 2 foll 6th rows, then on 3 foll 4th rows, then on foll alt row, then at same edge on 2 foll rows, ending with **WS** facing for next row, **and at same time** dec 1 st at front slope edge of next and every foll 4th row. 56 [63: 70: 77] sts.
Place markers at beg of last row to denote base of armhole opening.
Dec 1 st at front slope edge **only** on 4th and every foll 4th row until 41 [47: 53: 59] sts rem.
Cont straight until left front matches back to beg of shoulder shaping, ending with RS facing for next row.
**Shape shoulder**
Cast off 10 [12: 13: 15] sts at beg of next row and 11 [12: 13: 15] sts at beg of 2 foll alt rows.
Work 1 row.
Cast off rem 9 [11: 14: 14] sts.

## RIGHT FRONT

Using 3¾mm (US 5) needles cast on 71 [77: 84: 90] sts.
**Row 1 (RS):** Knit.
**Row 2:** K1, P1, *K3, P1, rep from * to last 1 [3: 2: 0]

sts, K1 [3: 2: 0].

**Rows 3 to 6:** As rows 1 and 2, twice.

**Row 7:** Knit.

**Row 8:** *K3, P1, rep from * to last 3 [1: 0: 2] sts, K3 [1: 0: 2].

**Rows 9 to 12:** As rows 7 and 8, twice.

These 12 rows form patt.

Cont in patt until right front meas 18 [19: 20: 22] cm, ending with RS facing for next row.

**Place belt opening**

**Next row (RS):** K to last 11 sts and turn, leaving rem sts on a holder.

Work in patt on these 60 [66: 73: 79] sts only for a further 14 rows, ending with **WS** facing for next row.

Break yarn and leave sts on a 2nd holder.

Return to sts left on first holder, rejoin yarn with RS facing and K to end.

Work in patt on these 11 sts only for a further 14 rows, ending with **WS** facing for next row.

**Join sections**

**Next row (WS):** Patt 11 sts of last section, then patt 60 [66: 73: 79] sts on 2nd holder. 71 [77: 84: 90] sts.

**Shape front slope**

Keeping patt correct, dec 1 st at beg of next and foll 13 [12: 12: 11] alt rows. 57 [64: 71: 78] sts.

Complete to match left front, reversing shapings.

**MAKING UP**

Press as described on the information page.

Join both shoulder seams using back stitch, or mattress stitch if preferred.

See information page for finishing instructions, leaving side seams open above markers.

**Belt**

Using 3¾mm (US 5) needles cast on 9 sts.

Work in g st until belt meas 110 [120: 130: 140] cm. Cast off.

Using photograph as a guide, thread belt through belt openings and tie ends at front.

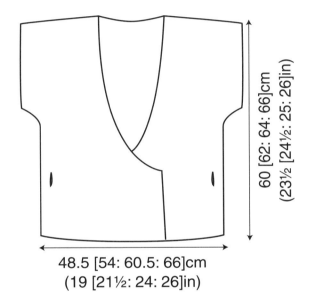

60 [62: 64: 66]cm
(23½ [24½: 25: 26]in)

48.5 [54: 60.5: 66]cm
(19 [21½: 24: 26]in)

# Chicory

main image page 46

## SIZE

| 8 | 10 | 12 | 14 | 16 | 18 | 20 | 22 | |
|---|---|---|---|---|---|---|---|---|
| To fit bust | | | | | | | | |
| 81 | 86 | 91 | 97 | 102 | 107 | 112 | 117 | cm |
| 32 | 34 | 36 | 38 | 40 | 42 | 44 | 46 | in |

## YARN

**Rowan Purleife Organic Wool DK**

10  10  10  11  12  12  13  13 x 50gm
(photographed in Horsetail 605)

## NEEDLES

1 pair 3¾mm (no 9) (US 5) needles
1 pair 4mm (no 8) (US 6) needles
3.50mm (no 9) (US E4) crochet hook

**EXTRAS** - 130 [130: 140: 140: 150: 150: 160: 160] cm of 15 mm (5/8 in) wide velvet ribbon

## TENSION

22 sts and 30 rows to 10 cm measured over patt using 4mm (US 6) needles.

**Pattern note**: When working patt from chart, do NOT work the inc ("yfwd") unless there are sufficient sts to work the corresponding dec ("K2tog", "sl 1, K1, psso" or "sl 1, K2tog, psso").

## BACK

Using 3¾mm (US 5) needles cast on 111 [115: 119: 125: 133: 139: 145: 153] sts.
**Row 1 (RS):** K1, *P1, K1, rep from * to end.
**Row 2:** As row 1.
These 2 rows form moss st.
Work in moss st for a further 3 rows, ending with **WS** facing for next row.
Change to 4mm (US 6) needles.
Beg with a P row, work in st st for 5 rows, ending with RS facing for next row.
Beg and ending rows as indicated and repeating the 100 row patt rep throughout, cont in patt from chart as folls:
Dec 1 st at each end of 3rd and every foll 10th row until 93 [97: 101: 107: 115: 121: 127: 135] sts rem.
Cont straight until back meas 45 [45: 44: 47: 46: 48: 47: 49] cm, ending with RS facing for next row.
### Shape armholes
Keeping patt correct, cast off 3 [4: 4: 5: 5: 6: 6: 7] sts at beg of next 2 rows. 87 [89: 93: 97: 105: 109: 115: 121] sts.
Dec 1 st at each end of next 3 [3: 5: 5: 7: 7: 9: 9] rows, then on foll 4 [4: 3: 3: 4: 4: 3: 5] alt rows.
73 [75: 77: 81: 83: 87: 91: 93] sts.**
Cont straight until armhole meas 18 [18: 19: 19: 20: 20: 21: 21] cm, ending with RS facing for next row.
### Shape shoulders and back neck
**Next row (RS):** Cast off 5 [6: 6: 7: 7: 7: 8: 8] sts, patt until there are 17 [17: 18: 19: 19: 21: 22: 23] sts on right needle and turn, leaving rem sts on a holder.
Work each side of neck separately.
Cast off 3 sts at beg of next row, 5 [6: 6: 7: 7: 7: 8: 8] sts at beg of foll row, then 3 sts at beg of next row.
Cast off rem 6 [5: 6: 6: 6: 8: 8: 9] sts.
With RS facing, rejoin yarn to rem sts, cast off centre 29 [29: 29: 29: 31: 31: 31: 31] sts, patt to end.
Complete to match first side, reversing shapings.

## FRONT

Work as given for back to **.
Work 7 [7: 9: 9: 7: 7: 9: 5] rows, ending with RS facing for next row.
### Shape neck
**Next row (RS):** Patt 28 [29: 30: 33: 33: 35: 38: 39] sts and turn, leaving rem sts on a holder.
Work each side of neck separately.
Dec 1 st at neck edge of next 6 rows, then on foll 4 [4: 4: 5: 5: 5: 6: 6] alt rows, then on 2 foll 4th rows.
16 [17: 18: 20: 20: 22: 24: 25] sts.
Cont straight until front matches back to beg of shoulder shaping, ending with RS facing for next row.
### Shape shoulder
Cast off 5 [6: 6: 7: 7: 7: 8: 8] sts at beg of next and foll alt row.
Work 1 row.
Cast off rem 6 [5: 6: 6: 6: 8: 8: 9] sts.
With RS facing, rejoin yarn to rem sts, cast off centre

17 [17: 17: 15: 17: 17: 15: 15] sts, patt to end.
Complete to match first side, reversing shapings.
## SLEEVES
Using 3¾mm (US 5) needles cast on 53 [53: 55: 55: 57: 57: 59: 59] sts.
Work in moss st as given for back for 5 rows, ending with **WS** facing for next row.
Change to 4mm (US 6) needles.
Beg with a P row, work in st st for 5 rows, inc 1 st at each end of 2nd of these rows and ending with RS facing for next row. 55 [55: 57: 57: 59: 59: 61: 61] sts.
Beg and ending rows as indicated and repeating the 100 row patt rep throughout, cont in patt from chart as folls:
Inc 1 st at each end of 3rd and every foll 6th row to 63 [71: 71: 79: 77: 85: 91: 99] sts, then on every foll 8th [8th: 8th: 8th: 8th: 8th: 8th: -] row until there are 85 [87: 89: 91: 93: 95: 97: -] sts, taking inc sts into patt.
Cont straight until sleeve meas 44 [44: 45: 45: 46: 46:

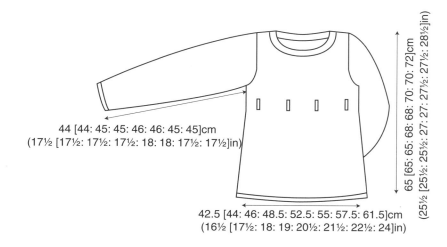

44 [44: 45: 45: 46: 46: 45: 45]cm
(17½ [17½: 17½: 17½: 18: 18: 17½: 17½]in)

65 [65: 65: 68: 68: 70: 70: 72]cm
(25½ [25½: 25½: 27: 27: 27½: 27½: 28½]in)

42.5 [44: 46: 48.5: 52.5: 55: 57.5: 61.5]cm
(16½ [17½: 18: 19: 20½: 21½: 22½: 24]in)

45: 45] cm, ending with RS facing for next row.

**Shape top**

Keeping patt correct, cast off 3 [4: 4: 5: 5: 6: 6: 7] sts at beg of next 2 rows. 79 [79: 81: 81: 83: 83: 85: 85] sts.

Dec 1 st at each end of next 5 rows, then on every foll alt row to 63 sts, then on foll 15 rows, ending with RS facing for next row. 33 sts.

Cast off 5 sts at beg of next 2 rows.

Cast off rem 23 sts.

**MAKING UP**

Press as described on the information page.

Join right shoulder seam using back stitch, or mattress stitch if preferred.

**Neckband**

With RS facing and using 3¾mm (US 5) needles, pick up and knit 34 [34: 34: 36: 36: 36: 38: 38] sts down left side of neck, 17 [17: 17: 15: 17: 17: 15: 15] sts from front, 34 [34: 34: 36: 36: 36: 38: 38] sts up right side of neck, then 42 [42: 42: 42: 44: 44: 44: 44] sts from back.

127 [127: 127: 129: 133: 133: 135: 135] sts.

Work in moss st as given for back for 4 rows, ending with **WS** facing for next row.

Cast off in moss st (on **WS**).

See information page for finishing instructions, setting in sleeves using the set-in method.

**Ribbon carriers (make 8)**

Using 3.50mm (US E4) crochet hook, make 7 chain and fasten off.

Using photograph as a guide, sew 4 ribbon carriers onto front, and 4 onto back - position carriers approx 12 cm below armhole and evenly spaced around garment. Thread ribbon through carriers and tie ends in a bow as in photograph.

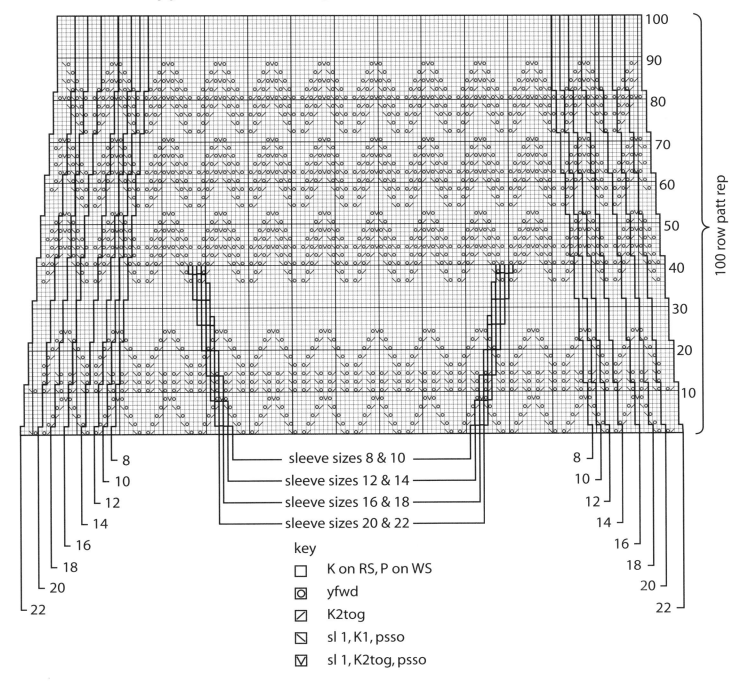

100 row patt rep

sleeve sizes 8 & 10
sleeve sizes 12 & 14
sleeve sizes 16 & 18
sleeve sizes 20 & 22

8
10
12
14
16
18
20
22

8
10
12
14
16
18
20
22

key

☐  K on RS, P on WS

◉  yfwd

⧄  K2tog

⧅  sl 1, K1, psso

⊠  sl 1, K2tog, psso

# Comfrey 🍃🍃

main image page 28

## SIZE

| 8 | 10 | 12 | 14 | 16 | 18 | 20 | 22 | |
|---|----|----|----|----|----|----|----|---|
| To fit bust | | | | | | | | |
| 81 | 86 | 91 | 97 | 102 | 107 | 112 | 117 | cm |
| 32 | 34 | 36 | 38 | 40 | 42 | 44 | 46 | in |

## YARN

**Rowan Purelife Organic Wool DK**

| 8 | 8 | 9 | 9 | 10 | 11 | 11 | 12 | x50gm |
|---|---|---|---|----|----|----|----|-------|

(photographed in Onion 607)

## NEEDLES

1 pair 3 1/4mm (no 10) (US 3) needles
1 pair 4mm (no 8) (US 6) needles
4.00mm (no 8) (US G6) crochet hook

**BUTTONS** – 8 x 00416

## TENSION

22 sts and 30 rows to 10 cm measured over st st using 4mm (US 6) needles.

## UK CROCHET ABBREVIATIONS

**ch** = chain; **ss** = slip stitch.

## BACK

Using 3 1/4mm (US 3) needles cast on 93 [97: 101: 107: 115: 121: 127: 135] sts.
**Row 1 (RS):** K1, *P1, K1, rep from * to end.
**Row 2:** P1, *K1, P1, rep from * to end.
These 2 rows form rib.
Work in rib for a further 22 rows, ending with RS facing for next row.
Change to 4mm (US 6) needles.
Beg with a K row, work in st st until back meas 34 [34: 33: 36: 35: 37: 36: 38] cm, ending with RS facing for next row.
**Shape armholes**
Cast off 3 [4: 4: 5: 5: 6: 6: 7] sts at beg of next 2 rows. 87 [89: 93: 97: 105: 109: 115: 121] sts.
Dec 1 st at each end of next 3 [3: 5: 5: 7: 7: 9: 9] rows, then on foll 4 [4: 3: 3: 4: 4: 3: 5] alt rows. 73 [75: 77: 81: 83: 87: 91: 93] sts.
Cont straight until armhole meas 18 [18: 19: 19: 20: 20: 21: 21] cm, ending with RS facing for next row.
**Shape shoulders and back neck**
**Next row (RS):** Cast off 6 [6: 7: 7: 7: 8: 9: 9] sts, K until there are 18 [19: 19: 21: 21: 22: 23: 24] sts on right needle and turn, leaving rem sts on a holder.
Work each side of neck separately.
Cast off 3 sts at beg of next row, 6 [6: 7: 7: 7: 8: 9: 9] sts at beg of foll row, then 3 sts at beg of next row.
Cast off rem 6 [7: 6: 8: 8: 8: 8: 9] sts.
With RS facing, rejoin yarn to rem sts, cast off centre 25 [25: 25: 25: 27: 27: 27: 27] sts, K to end.
Complete to match first side, reversing shapings.

## LEFT FRONT

Using 3 1/4mm (US 3) needles cast on 46 [48: 50: 52: 56: 60: 62: 66] sts.
**Row 1 (RS):** *K1, P1, rep from * to last 2 sts, K2.
**Row 2:** *K1, P1, rep from * to end.
These 2 rows form rib.

Work in rib for a further 22 rows, inc 0 [0: 0: 1: 1: 0: 1: 1] st at end of last row and ending with RS facing for next row. 46 [48: 50: 53: 57: 60: 63: 67] sts.
Change to 4mm (US 6) needles.
**Row 1 (RS):** K to last 14 sts, (P1, K1) 4 times, P1, K5.
**Row 2:** Purl.
These 2 rows form patt.
Cont in patt until left front matches back to beg of armhole shaping, ending with RS facing for next row.
**Shape armhole**
Keeping patt correct, cast off 3 [4: 4: 5: 5: 6: 6: 7] sts at beg of next row. 43 [44: 46: 48: 52: 54: 57: 60] sts.
Work 1 row.
Dec 1 st at armhole edge of next 3 [3: 5: 5: 7: 7: 9: 9] rows, then on foll 4 [4: 3: 3: 4: 4: 3: 5] alt rows. 36 [37: 38: 40: 41: 43: 45: 46] sts.
Cont straight until 21 [21: 21: 23: 23: 23: 25: 25] rows less have been worked than on back to beg of shoulder shaping, ending with **WS** facing for next row.
**Shape neck**
Keeping patt correct, cast off 9 [9: 9: 8: 9: 9: 8: 8] sts at beg of next row. 27 [28: 29: 32: 32: 34: 37: 38] sts.
Dec 1 st at neck edge of next 5 rows, then on foll 3 [3: 3: 4: 4: 4: 5: 5] alt rows, then on foll 4th row. 18 [19: 20: 22: 22: 24: 26: 27] sts.
Work 5 rows, ending with RS facing for next row.
**Shape shoulder**
Cast off 6 [6: 7: 7: 7: 8: 9: 9] sts at beg of next and foll alt row.
Work 1 row.
Cast off rem 6 [7: 6: 8: 8: 8: 8: 9] sts.

## RIGHT FRONT

Using 3 1/4mm (US 3) needles cast on 46 [48: 50: 52: 56: 60: 62: 66] sts.
**Row 1 (RS):** K2, *P1, K1, rep from * to end.
**Row 2:** *P1, K1, rep from * to end.

These 2 rows form rib.
Work in rib for a further 22 rows, inc 0 [0: 0: 1: 1: 0: 1: 1] st at beg of last row and ending with RS facing for next row. 46 [48: 50: 53: 57: 60: 63: 67] sts.
Change to 4mm (US 6) needles.
**Row 1 (RS):** K5, P1, (K1, P1) 4 times, K to end.
**Row 2:** Purl.
These 2 rows form patt.
Complete to match left front, reversing shapings.

## SLEEVES

Using 3 1/4mm (US 3) needles cast on 37 [37: 39: 39: 41: 41: 43: 43] sts.
Work in rib as given for back for 24 rows, ending with RS facing for next row.
Change to 4mm (US 6) needles.
Beg with a K row, work in st st, shaping sides by inc 1 st at each end of 3rd and every foll 4th row to 51 [57: 57: 63: 61: 67: 73: 79] sts, then on every foll 6th row until there are 75 [77: 79: 81: 83: 85: 87: 89] sts.
Cont straight until sleeve meas 45 [45: 46: 46: 47: 47: 46: 46] cm, ending with RS facing for next row.
**Shape top**
Cast off 3 [4: 4: 5: 5: 6: 6: 7] sts at beg of next 2 rows. 69 [69: 71: 71: 73: 73: 75: 75] sts.
Dec 1 st at each end of next 3 rows, then on every foll alt row to 51 sts, then on foll 11 rows, ending with RS facing for next row. 29 sts.
Cast off 5 sts at beg of next 2 rows.
Cast off rem 19 sts.

## MAKING UP

Press as described on the information page.
Join both shoulder seams using back stitch, or mattress stitch if preferred.
**Button band**
With RS facing and using 3 1/4mm (US 3) needles, beg at neck shaping, pick up and knit 113 [113: 113: 119:

119: 119: 119: 127] sts evenly down left front opening edge to cast-on edge.

**Row 1 (WS):** K1, *P1, K1, rep from * to end.

**Row 2:** K2, *P1, K1, rep from * to last st, K1.

These 2 rows form rib.

Work in rib for a further 2 rows, ending with **WS** facing for next row.

Cast off in rib (on **WS**).

**Buttonhole band**

With RS facing and using 3 1/4mm (US 3) needles, beg at cast-on edge, pick up and knit 113 [113: 113: 119: 119: 119: 119: 127] sts evenly up right front opening edge to neck shaping.

Work in rib as given for button band for 1 row, ending with RS facing for next row.

**Row 2 (RS):** Rib 4 [4: 4: 3: 3: 3: 3: 4], *yrn, work 2 tog (to make a buttonhole), rib 13 [13: 13: 14: 14: 14: 14: 15], rep from * 6 times more, yrn, work 2 tog (to make 8th buttonhole), rib 2.

Work in rib for a further 2 rows, ending with **WS** facing for next row.

Cast off in rib (on **WS**).

**Neckband**

With RS facing and using 3 1/4mm (US 3) needles, beg and ending at cast-off edges of bands, pick up and knit 35 [35: 35: 36: 37: 37: 38: 38] sts up right side of neck, 37 [37: 37: 37: 39: 39: 39: 39] sts from back, then 35 [35: 35: 36: 37: 37: 38: 38] sts down left side of neck.

107 [107: 107: 109: 113: 113: 115: 115] sts.

Cast off knitwise (on **WS**) but do NOT fasten off.

Slip rem st onto 4.00mm (US G6) crochet hook and work ruffle edging as folls: 1 ss into last cast-off st, *3 ch, miss 1 cast-off st, 1 ss into next cast-off st, rep from * to end.

Fasten off.

**Ruffles (all 10 alike)**

With RS facing, attach yarn to P st of patt nearest front opening edge at top of rib and work up this vertical line of P sts as folls: 1 ss into this P st, *3 ch, 1 ss into P st 2 rows above, rep from * to upper edge.

Fasten off.

Work ruffles up other 9 vertical P st lines in same way. See information page for finishing instructions, setting in sleeves using the set-in method.

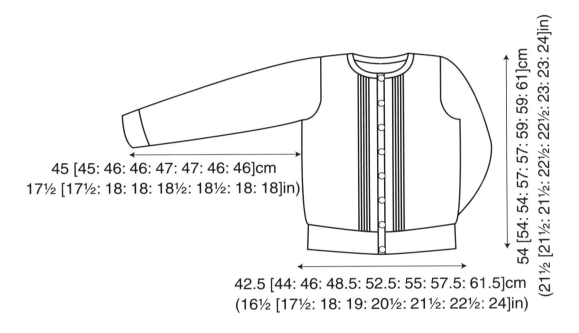

45 [45: 46: 46: 47: 47: 46: 46]cm
17½ [17½: 18: 18: 18½: 18½: 18: 18]in)

42.5 [44: 46: 48.5: 52.5: 55: 57.5: 61.5]cm
(16½ [17½: 18: 19: 20½: 21½: 22½: 24]in)

54 [54: 54: 57: 57: 59: 59: 61]cm
(21½ [21½: 21½: 22½: 22½: 23: 23: 24]in)

# Lovage
main image page 4

### SIZE

| 8 | 10 | 12 | 14 | 16 | 18 | 20 | 22 | |
|---|----|----|----|----|----|----|----|---|
| To fit bust | | | | | | | | |
| 81 | 86 | 91 | 97 | 102 | 107 | 112 | 117 | in |
| 32 | 34 | 36 | 38 | 40 | 42 | 44 | 46 | cm |

### YARN

**Rowan Purelife Organic Wool DK**

| 7 | 7 | 7 | 8 | 8 | 9 | 9 | 10 | x50gm |
|---|---|---|---|---|---|---|----|-------|

(photographed in Black Tea 603)

### NEEDLES

1 pair 3¾mm (no 9) (US 5) needles
1 pair 4mm (no 8) (US 6) needles
3¾mm (no 9) (US 5) circular needle
Cable needle

### TENSION

22 sts and 30 rows to 10 cm measured over rev st st using 4mm (US 6) needles.

### SPECIAL ABBREVIATIONS

**Cr3R** = slip next st onto cable needle and leave at back of work, K2, then P1 from cable needle;
**Cr3L** = slip next 2 sts onto cable needle and leave at front of work, P1, then K2 from cable needle;
**C4B** = slip next 2 sts onto cable needle and leave at back of work, K2, then K2 from cable needle;
**C4F** = slip next 2 sts onto cable needle and leave at front of work, K2, then K2 from cable needle.

### BACK

Using 3¾mm (US 5) needles cast on 92 [96: 102: 108: 114: 122: 128: 134] sts.
**Row 1 (RS):** K0 [1: 0: 0: 0: 0: 1: 0], P1 [2: 2: 1: 0: 0: 2: 2], *K2, P2, rep from * to last 3 [1: 0: 3: 2: 2: 1: 0] sts, K2 [1: 0: 2: 2: 2: 1: 0], P1 [0: 0: 1: 0: 0: 0: 0].
**Row 2:** P0 [1: 0: 0: 0: 0: 1: 0], K1 [2: 2: 1: 0: 0: 2: 2], *P2, K2, rep from * to last 3 [1: 0: 3: 2: 2: 1: 0] sts, P2 [1: 0: 2: 2: 2: 1: 0], K1 [0: 0: 1: 0: 0: 0: 0].
These 2 rows form rib.
Cont in rib until back meas 12 cm, ending with **WS** facing for next row.
**Next row (WS):** Rib 0 [2: 5: 8: 11: 5: 8: 11], (M1, rib 1, M1, rib 6, M1, rib 1, M1, rib 2) 0 [0: 0: 0: 0: 1: 1: 1] times, *rib 6, M1, rib 2, M1, rib 8, M1, rib 1, M1, rib 6, M1, rib 1, M1, rib 2, rep from * to last 14 [16: 19: 22: 25: 3: 6: 9] sts, (rib 6, M1, rib 2, M1) 1 [1: 1: 1: 1: 0: 0: 0] times, rib 6 [8: 11: 14: 17: 3: 6: 9].
112 [116: 122: 128: 134: 150: 156: 162] sts.
Change to 4mm (US 6) needles.
Now work in patt, placing cable panels as folls:
**Row 1 (RS):** P0 [2: 5: 8: 11: 3: 6: 9], (work next 16 sts as row 1 of cable panel A) 0 [0: 0: 0: 0: 1: 1: 1] times, *P4, work next 8 sts as row 1 of cable panel B, P4, work next 16 sts as row 1 of cable panel A, rep from * to last 16 [18: 21: 24: 27: 3: 6: 9] sts, (P4, work next 8 sts as row 1 of cable panel B) 1 [1: 1: 1: 1: 0: 0: 0] times, P4 [6: 9: 12: 15: 3: 6: 9].
**Row 2:** K0 [2: 5: 8: 11: 3: 6: 9], (work next 16 sts as row 2 of cable panel A) 0 [0: 0: 0: 0: 1: 1: 1] times, *K4, work next 8 sts as row 2 of cable panel B, K4, work next 16 sts as row 2 of cable panel A, rep from * to last 16 [18: 21: 24: 27: 3: 6: 9] sts, (K4, work next 8 sts as row 2 of cable panel B) 1 [1: 1: 1: 1: 0: 0: 0] times, K4 [6: 9: 12: 15: 3: 6: 9].
These 2 rows set position of cable panels with rev st st between and at sides.
Work in patt for a further 8 rows, ending with RS facing

for next row.
Keeping patt correct, dec 1 st at each end of next and 3 foll 8th rows. 104 [108: 114: 120: 126: 142: 148: 154] sts.
Cont straight until back meas 30 [30: 29: 32: 31: 33: 32: 34] cm, ending with RS facing for next row.**
Inc 1 st at each end of next and 3 foll 10th rows, taking inc sts into patt.
112 [116: 122: 128: 134: 150: 156: 162] sts.
Work 23 rows, ending with RS facing for next row. (Back should meas 48 [48: 47: 50: 49: 51: 50: 52] cm.)
**Shape armholes**
Keeping patt correct, cast off 5 [6: 6: 7: 7: 8: 8: 9] sts at beg of next 2 rows.
102 [104: 110: 114: 120: 134: 140: 144] sts.
Dec 1 st at each end of next 5 [5: 7: 7: 7: 9: 11: 11] rows, then on foll 5 [5: 5: 5: 5: 9: 7: 8] alt rows.
82 [84: 86: 90: 96: 98: 104: 106] sts.
Cont straight until armhole meas 19 [19: 20: 20: 21: 21: 22: 22] cm, ending with RS facing for next row.
**Shape back neck**
**Next row (RS):** Patt 14 [15: 16: 18: 20: 21: 24: 25] sts and turn, leaving rem sts on a holder.
Work each side of neck separately.
Keeping patt correct, cast off 6 sts at beg of next row, and 4 sts at beg of foll alt row.
4 [5: 6: 8: 10: 11: 14: 15] sts.
Dec 1 st at neck edge of next 2 rows, ending with RS facing for next row.
**Shape shoulder**
Cast off rem 2 [3: 4: 6: 8: 9: 12: 13] sts.
With RS facing, rejoin yarn to rem sts, cast off centre 54 [54: 54: 54: 56: 56: 56: 56] sts, patt to end.
Complete to match first side, reversing shapings.

### FRONT

Work as given for back to **.
Inc 1 st at each end of next row. 106 [110: 116: 122: 128: 144: 150: 156] sts.

Work 7 rows, ending with RS facing for next row.
**Divide for neck**
**Next row (RS):** Patt 53 [55: 58: 61: 64: 72: 75: 78] sts and turn, leaving rem sts on a holder.
Work each side of neck separately.
Keeping patt correct, dec 1 st at neck edge of 2nd and foll 21 alt rows **and at same time** inc 1 st at side seam edge of 2nd and 2 foll 10th rows. 34 [36: 39: 42: 45: 53: 56: 59] sts.
Work 1 row, ending with RS facing for next row.
**Shape armhole**
Keeping patt correct, cast off 5 [6: 6: 7: 7: 8: 8: 9] sts at beg and dec 1 st at end of next row.
28 [29: 32: 34: 37: 44: 47: 49] sts.
Work 1 row.
Dec 1 st at armhole edge of next 5 [5: 7: 7: 7: 9: 11: 11] rows, then on foll 5 [5: 5: 5: 5: 9: 7: 8] alt rows **and**

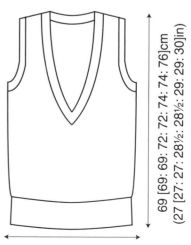

69 [69: 69: 72: 72: 74: 74: 76]cm
(27 [27: 27: 28½: 28½: 29: 29: 30]in)

42 [43.5: 46.5: 49: 52: 55.5: 58: 61]cm
(16½ [17: 18½: 19½: 20½: 22: 23: 24]in)

**at same time** dec 1 st at neck edge of next and foll 4 [4: 3: 3: 3: 3: 2: 2] alt rows, then on every foll 4th row. 12 [13: 14: 16: 19: 17: 21: 22] sts.

Dec 1 st at neck edge **only** on 2nd [2nd: 2nd: 2nd: 2nd: 4th: 4th: 2nd] and every foll 4th row until 2 [3: 4: 6: 8: 9: 12: 13] sts rem.

Cont straight until front matches back to shoulder cast-off, ending with RS facing for next row.

**Shape shoulder**

Cast off rem 2 [3: 4: 6: 8: 9: 12: 13] sts.

With RS facing, rejoin yarn to rem sts, patt to end.

Complete to match first side, reversing shapings.

**MAKING UP**

Press as described on the information page.

Join both shoulder seams using back stitch, or mattress stitch if preferred.

**Neckband**

With RS facing and using 3¾mm (US 5) circular needle, pick up and knit 85 [85: 89: 89: 93: 93: 97: 97] sts down left side of neck, place marker on needle, 85 [85: 89: 89: 93: 93: 97: 97] sts up right side of neck, then 62 [62: 62: 62: 66: 66: 66: 66] sts from back.

232 [232: 240: 240: 252: 252: 260: 260] sts.

**Round 1 (RS):** *K2, P2, rep from * to end.

This round sets position of rib.

Keeping rib correct, cont as folls:

**Round 2**: Rib to within 2 sts of marker, K2tog, slip marker onto right needle, sl 1, K1, psso, rib to end.

**Round 3:** Rib to within 1 st of marker, K2 (marker is between these 2 sts), rib to end.

Rep rounds 2 and 3 twice more, then round 2 again. 224 [224: 232: 232: 244: 244: 252: 252] sts.

Cast off in rib.

**Armhole borders (both alike)**

With RS facing and using 3¾mm (US 5) needles, pick up and knit 102 [106: 110: 114: 118: 122: 126: 130] sts evenly all round armhole edge.

**Row 1 (WS):** P2, *K2, P2, rep from * to end.

**Row 2:** K2, *P2, K2, rep from * to end.

Rep last 2 rows twice more, ending with **WS** facing for next row.

Cast off in rib (on **WS**).

See information page for finishing instructions.

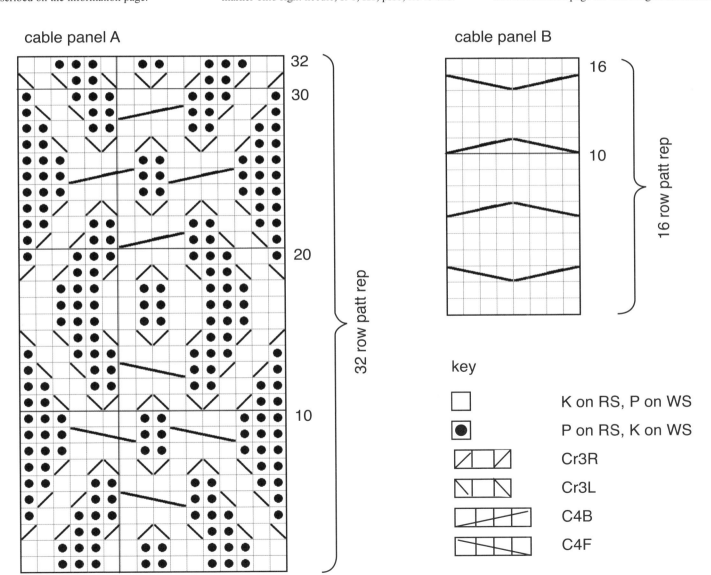

cable panel A

cable panel B

32 row patt rep

16 row patt rep

key

| | |
|---|---|
| ☐ | K on RS, P on WS |
| ⊡ | P on RS, K on WS |
| ◿ | Cr3R |
| ◺ | Cr3L |
| ⬗ | C4B |
| ⬖ | C4F |

# Marjoram

main image page 26

## SIZE

|  | S | M | L | XL |  |
|---|---|---|---|---|---|
| To fit bust |  |  |  |  |  |
|  | 81-86 | 91-97 | 102-107 | 112-117 | cm |
|  | 32-34 | 36-38 | 40-42 | 44-46 | in |

## YARN

**Rowan Purelife Organic Wool DK**

|  | 8 | 9 | 9 | 10 | x 50gm |
|---|---|---|---|---|---|

(photographed in Tanin 604)

## NEEDLES

1 pair 3¾mm (no 9) (US 5) needles
1 pair 4mm (no 8) (US 6) needles

## TENSION

22 sts and 30 rows to 10 cm measured over rib when pressed using 4mm (US 6) needles.

**BODY** (worked in one piece from cuff to cuff)

Using 4mm (US 6) needles cast on 88 [92: 96: 96] sts.

**Row 1 (RS):** K2 [0: 0: 0], P4 [0: 2: 2], *K4, P4, rep from * to last 2 [4: 6: 6] sts, K2 [4: 4: 4], P0 [0: 2: 2].

**Row 2:** P2 [0: 0: 0], K4 [0: 2: 2], *P4, K4, rep from * to last 2 [4: 6: 6] sts, P2 [4: 4: 4], K0 [0: 2: 2].

These 2 rows form rib.

Cont in rib, inc 1 st at each end of next and foll 9 [14: 16: 26] alt rows, then on every foll 4th row until there are 140 [150: 158: 168] sts, taking inc sts into rib.

Work 3 rows, ending with RS facing for next row. (Work should meas 29 [30: 31: 31] cm.)

**Shape body**

Place markers at both ends of last row to denote base of underarm/side seam.

Cont straight until work meas 6 [8.5: 11: 14] cm from markers, ending with RS facing for next row.

**Divide for neck**

**Next row (RS):** Rib 69 [74: 78: 83], K1 and turn, leaving rem sts on a holder.

Work each side of neck separately.

**Next row (WS):** K1, rib to end.

**Next row:** Rib to last st, K1.

These 2 rows set the sts.

Cont as set until work meas 25 [25: 26: 26] cm from beg of neck opening, ending with **WS** facing for next row.

Break yarn and leave sts on another holder.

With RS facing, rejoin yarn to rem sts and cont as folls:

**Next row (RS):** K1, rib to end.

**Next row:** Rib to last st, K1.

These 2 rows set the sts.

Cont as set until work meas 25 [25: 26: 26] cm from beg of neck opening, ending with **WS** facing for next row.

**Join sections**

**Next row (WS):** Rib 70 [75: 79: 84], then rib across 70 [75: 79: 84] sts on holder. 140 [150: 158: 168] sts.

Cont straight in rib across all sts until work meas 6 [8.5: 11: 14] cm from joining row, ending with RS facing for next row.

**Shape second sleeve**

Place markers at both ends of last row to denote base of other underarm/side seam.

Cont in rib, dec 1 st at each end of 5th and 16 [14: 14: 9] foll 4th rows, then on every foll alt row until 88 [92: 96: 96] sts rem.

Work 1 row, ending with RS facing for next row.

Cast off in rib.

**MAKING UP**

Press as described on the information page.

**Hembands (both alike)**

With RS facing and using 3¾mm (US 5) needles, pick up and knit 82 [90: 106: 118] sts evenly along one straight row-end edge between markers.

**Row 1 (WS):** P2, *K2, P2, rep from * to end.

**Row 2:** K2, *P2, K2, rep from * to end.

These 2 rows form rib.

Cont in rib until hemband meas 16 cm from pick-up row, ending with RS facing for next row.

Cast off in rib.

**Cuffs (both alike)**

With RS facing and using 3¾mm (US 5) needles, pick up and knit 88 [88: 96: 96] sts evenly along cast-on (or cast-off) edge of body.

**Row 1 (WS):** P2, *(K2tog) twice, (P2tog) twice, rep from * to last 6 sts, (K2tog) twice, P2.

46 [46: 50: 50] sts.

Beg with row 2, work in rib as given for hemband until cuff meas 10 cm from pick-up row, ending with RS facing for next row.

Cast off in rib.

See information page for finishing instructions.

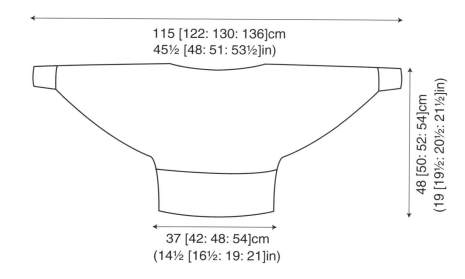

115 [122: 130: 136]cm
45½ [48: 51: 53½]in)

48 [50: 52: 54]cm
(19 [19½: 20½: 21½]in)

37 [42: 48: 54]cm
(14½ [16½: 19: 21]in)

# Chervil

main image page 21

## SIZE

|  | S | M | L | XL |  |
|---|---|---|---|---|---|
| To fit bust |  |  |  |  |  |
|  | 81-86 | 91-97 | 102-107 | 112-117 | cm |
|  | 32-34 | 36-38 | 40-42 | 44-46 | in |

## YARN

**Rowan Purelife Organic Wool DK**

| 12 | 13 | 13 | 14 | x 50gm |
|---|---|---|---|---|

(photographed in Black Tea 603)

## NEEDLES

1 pair 3¾mm (no 9) (US 5) needles
1 pair 4mm (no 8) (US 6) needles

## TENSION

21 sts and 44 rows to 10 cm measured over patt
using 4mm (US 6) needles.

## SPECIAL ABBREVIATIONS

**K1 below** = K into next st 1 row below st on left
needle, slipping st above off left needle at same time.

## BACK

Using 3¾mm (US 5) needles cast on 102 [114: 126: 138] sts.
**Row 1 (RS):** K2, *P2, K2, rep from * to end.
**Row 2:** P2, *K2, P2, rep from * to end.
These 2 rows form rib.
Cont in rib until back meas 12 cm, inc [dec: inc: inc]
1 st at end of last row and ending with **WS** facing for
next row. 103 [113: 127: 139] sts.
Change to 4mm (US 6) needles.
**Next row (WS):** Purl.
Now work in patt as folls:
**Row 1 (RS):** sl 1, *K1 below, P1, rep from * to last 2 sts,
K1 below, K1.
**Row 2:** sl 1, *P1, K1 below, rep from * to last 2 sts, P1, K1.
These 2 rows form patt.
Cont in patt until back meas 33 [34: 35: 36] cm, ending
with RS facing for next row.
### Shape for cap sleeves
Inc 1 st at each end of next and foll 8th row, then on 3
foll 6th rows, then on 4 foll 4th rows, then on foll 3 alt
rows, taking inc sts into patt and ending with **WS** facing
for next row. 127 [137: 151: 163] sts.
Place markers at both ends of last row to denote base of
armholes.
Cont straight until back meas 18 [19: 20: 21] cm from
markers, ending with RS facing for next row.
### Shape shoulders and back neck
**Next row (RS):** Cast off 8 [9: 10: 11] sts, patt until
there are 39 [43: 48: 53] sts on right needle and turn,
leaving rem sts on a holder.
Work each side of neck separately.
Keeping patt correct, dec 1 st at neck edge of next 6
rows **and at same time** cast off 8 [9: 10: 11] sts at beg
of 2nd and foll 2 [2: 1: 0] alt rows, then 0 [0: 11: 12] sts
at beg of foll 0 [0: 1: 2] alt rows.
Work 1 row.
Cast off rem 9 [10: 11: 12] sts.
With RS facing, rejoin yarn to rem sts, cast off centre

33 [33: 35: 35] sts, patt to end.
Complete to match first side, reversing shapings.

## FRONT

Work as given for back until 42 [42: 46: 46] rows less
have been worked than on back to beg of shoulder
shaping, ending with RS facing for next row.
### Shape neck
**Next row (RS):** Patt 56 [61: 68: 74] sts and turn,
leaving rem sts on a holder.
Work each side of neck separately.
Keeping patt correct, dec 1 st at neck edge of next 6
rows, then on foll 4 alt rows, then on 3 [3: 4: 4] foll
4th rows, then on 2 foll 6th rows. 41 [46: 52: 58] sts.
Work 3 rows, ending with RS facing for next row.
### Shape shoulder
Cast off 8 [9: 10: 11] sts at beg of next and foll 3 [3: 2:
1] alt rows, then 0 [0: 11: 12] sts at beg of foll 0 [0: 1:
2] alt rows.
Work 1 row.
Cast off rem 9 [10: 11: 12] sts.
With RS facing, rejoin yarn to rem sts, cast off centre
15 sts, patt to end.
Complete to match first side, reversing shapings.

## MAKING UP

Press as described on the information page.
Join right shoulder seam using back stitch, or mattress
stitch if preferred.
### Collar
With RS facing and using 3¾mm (US 5) needles, pick
up and knit 28 [28: 30: 30] sts down left side of neck,
15 sts from front, 28 [28: 30: 30] sts up right side of
neck, then 46 [46: 48: 48] sts from back.
117 [117: 123: 123] sts.
**Row 1 (WS of body, RS of collar):** K1, *P1, K1, rep
from * to end.
**Row 2:** P1, *K1, P1, rep from * to end.

Rep last 2 rows 3 times more.
**Row 9:** Inc in first st, *P1, inc in next st, rep from * to
end. 176 [176: 185: 185] sts.
**Row 10:** P2, *K1, P2, rep from * to end.
**Row 11:** K2, *P1, K2, rep from * to end.
Rep last 2 rows 3 times more.
**Row 18:** P2, *inc in next st, P2, rep from * to end.
234 [234: 246: 246] sts.
Beg with row 1, cont in rib as given for back until collar
meas 24 cm from pick-up row, ending with RS of collar
facing for next row.
Cast off in rib.
See information page for finishing instructions, leaving
side seams open above markers.

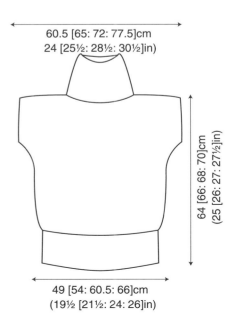

60.5 [65: 72: 77.5]cm
24 [25½: 28½: 30½]in)

64 [66: 68: 70]cm
(25 [26: 27: 27½]in)

49 [54: 60.5: 66]cm
(19½ [21½: 24: 26]in)

# Par-cel

main image page 8

## SIZE

| 8 | 10 | 12 | 14 | 16 | 18 | 20 | 22 | |
|---|----|----|----|----|----|----|----|---|
| To fit bust | | | | | | | | |
| 81 | 86 | 91 | 97 | 102 | 107 | 112 | 117 | cm |
| 32 | 34 | 36 | 38 | 40 | 42 | 44 | 46 | in |

## YARN

**Rowan Purleife Organic Wool DK**

| 11 | 12 | 12 | 13 | 14 | 14 | 15 | 16 | x 50gm |
|----|----|----|----|----|----|----|----|--------|

(photographed in Ivy 602)

## NEEDLES

1 pair 3¾mm (no 9) (US 5) needles
1 pair 4mm (no 8) (US 6) needles

**BUTTONS** - 10 x 00410 and 4 x 00408

## TENSION

22 sts and 30 rows to 10 cm measured over st st using 4mm (US 6) needles.

## BACK

Using 3¾mm (US 5) needles cast on 97 [101: 105: 113: 119: 125: 133: 139] sts.
**Row 1 (RS):** K1, *P1, K1, rep from * to end.
**Rows 2 and 3:** P1, *K1, P1, rep from * to end.
**Row 4:** As row 1.
These 4 rows form double moss st.
Work in double moss st for a further 6 rows, ending with RS facing for next row.
Change to 4mm (US 6) needles.
Beg with a K row, work in st st, shaping side seams by dec 1 st at each end of 5th and every foll 8th row until 83 [87: 91: 99: 105: 111: 119: 125] sts rem.
Work 15 rows, ending with RS facing for next row.
Inc 1 st at each end of next and every foll 6th row until there are 97 [101: 105: 113: 119: 125: 133: 139] sts.
Cont straight until back meas 41 [41: 40: 43: 42: 44: 43: 45] cm, ending with RS facing for next row.
**Shape armholes**
Cast off 3 [4: 4: 5: 5: 6: 6: 7] sts at beg of next 2 rows. 91 [93: 97: 103: 109: 113: 121: 125] sts.
Dec 1 st at each end of next 5 [5: 7: 7: 9: 9: 11: 11] rows, then on foll 4 [4: 3: 4: 4: 4: 4: 5] alt rows. 73 [75: 77: 81: 83: 87: 91: 93] sts.
Cont straight until armhole meas 18 [18: 19: 19: 20: 20: 21: 21] cm, ending with RS facing for next row.
**Shape shoulders and back neck**
**Next row (RS):** Cast off 5 [6: 6: 7: 7: 7: 8: 8] sts, K until there are 17 [17: 18: 19: 19: 21: 22: 23] sts on right needle and turn, leaving rem sts on a holder.
Work each side of neck separately.
Cast off 3 sts at beg of next row, 5 [6: 6: 7: 7: 7: 8: 8] sts at beg of foll row, then 3 sts at beg of next row.
Cast off rem 6 [5: 6: 6: 6: 8: 8: 9] sts.
With RS facing, rejoin yarn to rem sts, cast off centre 29 [29: 29: 29: 31: 31: 31: 31] sts, K to end.
Complete to match first side, reversing shapings.

## LEFT FRONT

Using 3¾mm (US 5) needles cast on 69 [71: 73: 77: 81: 83: 87: 91] sts.
Work in double moss st as given for back for 9 rows, ending with **WS** facing for next row.
**Row 10 (WS):** Patt 7 sts and slip these sts onto a holder, M1, patt to last 0 [0: 0: 0: 2: 0: 0: 2] sts, (work 2 tog) 0 [0: 0: 0: 1: 0: 0: 1] times.
63 [65: 67: 71: 74: 77: 81: 84] sts.
Change to 4mm (US 6) needles.
Beg with a K row, work in st st, shaping side seam by dec 1 st at beg of 5th and every foll 8th row until 56 [58: 60: 64: 67: 70: 74: 77] sts rem.
Work 15 rows, ending with RS facing for next row.
Inc 1 st at beg of next and every foll 6th row until there are 63 [65: 67: 71: 74: 77: 81: 84] sts.
Cont straight until left front matches back to beg of armhole shaping, ending with RS facing for next row.
**Shape armhole**
Cast off 3 [4: 4: 5: 5: 6: 6: 7] sts at beg of next row. 60 [61: 63: 66: 69: 71: 75: 77] sts.
Work 1 row.
Dec 1 st at armhole edge of next 5 [5: 7: 7: 9: 9: 11: 11] rows, then on foll 4 [4: 3: 4: 4: 4: 4: 5] alt rows. 51 [52: 53: 55: 56: 58: 60: 61] sts.
Cont straight until 23 [23: 23: 25: 25: 25: 27: 27] rows less have been worked than on back to beg of shoulder shaping, ending with **WS** facing for next row.
**Shape neck**
Cast off 24 [24: 24: 23: 24: 24: 23: 23] sts at beg of next row. 27 [28: 29: 32: 32: 34: 37: 38] sts.
Dec 1 st at neck edge of next 7 rows, then on foll 3 [3: 3: 4: 4: 4: 5: 5] alt rows, then on foll 4th row. 16 [17: 18: 20: 20: 22: 24: 25] sts.
Work 5 rows, ending with RS facing for next row.
**Shape shoulder**
Cast off 5 [6: 6: 7: 7: 7: 8: 8] sts at beg of next and foll alt row.

Work 1 row.
Cast off rem 6 [5: 6: 6: 6: 8: 8: 9] sts.
Mark positions for 3 pairs of buttons on left front - first pair to come 2 rows above last side seam dec, top pair to come 2 cm below neck shaping, and 3rd pair evenly spaced between.

## RIGHT FRONT

Using 3¾mm (US 5) needles cast on 69 [71: 73: 77: 81: 83: 87: 91] sts.
Work in double moss st as given for back for 9 rows, ending with **WS** facing for next row.
**Row 10 (WS):** (Work 2 tog) 0 [0: 0: 0: 1: 0: 0: 1] times, patt to last 7 sts, M1 and turn, leaving rem 7 sts on a holder. 63 [65: 67: 71: 74: 77: 81: 84] sts.
Change to 4mm (US 6) needles.
Beg with a K row, work in st st, shaping side seam by dec 1 st at end of 5th and every foll 8th row until 56 [58: 60: 64: 67: 70: 74: 77] sts rem.
Work 1 row, ending with RS facing for next row.
**Next row (buttonhole row) (RS):** K2, cast off 3 sts (to make first buttonhole of this pair - cast on 3 sts over these cast off sts on next row), K until there are 19 sts on right needle after cast-off, cast off 3 sts (to make 2nd buttonhole of this pair - cast on 3 sts over these cast off sts on next row), K to end.
Working a further 2 pairs of buttonholes in this way to correspond with positions marked for buttons on left front and noting that no further reference will be made to buttonholes, cont as folls:
Work 13 rows, ending with RS facing for next row.
Inc 1 st at end of next and every foll 6th row until there are 63 [65: 67: 71: 74: 77: 81: 84] sts.
Complete to match left front, reversing shapings.

## SLEEVES

Using 3¾mm (US 5) needles cast on 45 [45: 47: 47: 49: 49: 51: 51] sts.

Work in double moss st as given for back for 16 cm, ending with RS facing for next row.

Change to 4mm (US 6) needles.

Beg with a K row, work in st st, shaping sides by inc 1 st at each end of 3rd and every foll 4th row to 71 [77: 77: 83: 81: 87: 93: 99] sts, then on every foll 6th [6th: 6th: 6th: 6th: 6th: 6th: -] row until there are 85 [87: 89: 91: 93: 95: 97: -] sts.

Cont straight until sleeve meas 52 [52: 53: 53: 54: 54: 53: 53] cm, ending with RS facing for next row.

## Shape top

Cast off 3 [4: 4: 5: 5: 6: 6: 7] sts at beg of next 2 rows. 79 [79: 81: 81: 83: 83: 85: 85].

Dec 1 st at each end of next 5 rows, then on every foll alt row to 63 sts, then on foll 17 rows, ending with RS facing for next row. 29 sts.

Cast off 5 sts at beg of next 2 rows.

Cast off rem 19 sts.

## MAKING UP

Press as described on the information page.

Join both shoulder seams using back stitch, or mattress stitch if preferred.

## Left front band

Slip 7 sts from holder onto 3¾mm (US 5) needles and rejoin yarn with RS facing.

Cont in double moss st as set until band, when slightly stretched, fits up left front opening edge to neck shaping, ending with RS facing for next row.

Break yarn and leave sts on a holder.

## Right front band

Slip 7 sts from holder onto 3¾mm (US 5) needles and rejoin yarn with **WS** facing.

Cont in double moss st as set until band, when slightly stretched, fits up right front opening edge to neck shaping, ending with RS facing for next row. (**Note**: End after same patt row as on left front band.)

Do NOT break yarn.

Slip stitch bands in place.

## Neckband

With RS facing and using 3¾mm (US 5) needles, patt 7 sts of right front band, pick up and knit 47 [47: 47: 48: 49: 49: 50: 50] sts up right side of neck, 41 [41: 41: 41: 43: 43: 43: 43] sts from back, and 47 [47: 47: 48: 49: 49: 50: 50] sts down left side of neck, then patt 7 sts of left front band. 149 [149: 149: 151: 155: 155: 157: 157] sts.

Work in double moss st as set by bands for 8 rows, ending with **WS** facing for next row.

Cast off in patt (on **WS**).

## Pockets (make 2)

Using 3¾mm (US 5) needles cast on 29 sts.

Work in double moss st as given for back for 11 cm, ending with RS facing for next row.

**Next row (RS):** Patt 13 sts, cast off 3 sts (to make a buttonhole - cast on 3 sts over these cast off sts on next row), patt to end.

Cont in double moss st until pocket meas 13 cm, ending with **WS** facing for next row.

Cast off in patt (on **WS**).

## Belt loops (make 4)

Using 3¾mm (US 5) needles cast on 5 sts.

Work in double moss st as given for back for 18 rows, ending with RS facing for next row.

**Next row (RS):** K2tog, P1, K2tog tbl.

**Next row:** sl 1, K2tog, psso and fasten off.

## Belt

Using 3¾mm (US 5) needles cast on 7 sts.

Work in double moss st as given for back until belt meas 130 cm, ending with **WS** facing for next row.

Cast off in patt (on **WS**).

See information page for finishing instructions, setting in sleeves using the set-in method and reversing sleeve seam for first 13 cm. Fold 8 cm cuff to RS and secure in place by attaching a large button through both layers as in photograph.

Using photograph as a guide, sew pockets onto fronts. Attach large buttons to fronts to correspond with buttonholes in pockets.

Try on garment and mark waist position. Using photograph as a guide, sew straight ends of belt loops onto fronts and back just above waist level. Fold pointed end of belt loop down and secure in place by attaching a small button through both layers. Thread belt through belt loops.

Attach rem 6 large buttons to left front to correspond with buttonholes in right front - buttons nearest front opening edge should be attached just next to band seam.

44 [44: 45: 45: 46: 46: 45: 45]cm
(17½ [17½: 17½: 17½: 18: 18: 17½: 17½]in)

44 [46: 47.5: 51.5: 54: 57: 60.5: 63]cm
(17½ [18: 18½: 20½: 21½: 22½: 24: 25]in)

61 [61: 61: 64: 66: 66: 66: 68]cm
(24 [24: 24: 25: 26: 26: 26: 27]in)

# Parsley

main image page 24

**SIZE**

| 8 | 10 | 12 | 14 | 16 | 18 | 20 | 22 | |
|---|----|----|----|----|----|----|----|---|
| To fit bust | | | | | | | | |
| 81 | 86 | 91 | 97 | 102 | 107 | 112 | 117 | cm |
| 32 | 34 | 36 | 38 | 40 | 42 | 44 | 46 | in |

**YARN**

**Rowan Purleife Organic Wool DK**

7   7   7   8   8   9   9   9   x 50gm

(photographed in Buckthorn 606)

**NEEDLES**

1 pair 3¾mm (no 9) (US 5) needles
1 pair 4mm (no 8) (US 6) needles
3¾mm (no 9) (US 5) circular needle

**BUTTONS** – 2 x 00408

**TENSION**

21 sts and 30 rows to 10 cm measured over patt
using 4mm (US 6) needles.

## BACK

Using 3¾mm (US 5) needles cast on 85 [89: 93: 99:
105: 111: 117: 125] sts.

Work in g st for 12 rows, ending with RS facing for
next row.

Change to 4mm (US 6) needles.

**Row 1 (RS):** K1 [3: 1: 2: 1: 2: 1: 3], (K2tog, yfwd)
1 [1: 0: 1: 0: 1: 0: 1] times, *K1, yfwd, sl 1, K1,
psso, K1, K2tog, yfwd, rep from * to last 4 [6: 2: 5:
2: 5: 2: 6] sts, (K1, yfwd, sl 1, K1, psso) 1 [1: 0: 1:
0: 1: 0: 1] times, K1 [3: 2: 2: 2: 2: 2: 3].

**Row 2 and every foll alt row**: Purl.

**Rows 3 and 5**: As row 1.

**Row 7:** K0 [2: 1: 1: 1: 1: 1: 2], (K2tog, yfwd, K1) 1 [1:
0: 1: 0: 1: 0: 1] times, *K2, yfwd, sl 1, K2tog, psso,
yfwd, K1, rep from * to last 4 [6: 2: 5: 2: 5: 2: 6] sts,
(K2, yfwd, sl 1, K1, psso) 1 [1: 0: 1: 0: 1: 0: 1] times,
K0 [2: 1: 1: 2: 1: 2: 2].

**Row 9:** K1 [3: 1: 2: 1: 2: 1: 3], (yfwd, sl 1, K1, psso)
1 [1: 0: 1: 0: 1: 0: 1] times, *K1, K2tog, yfwd, K1,
yfwd, sl 1, K1, psso, rep from * to last 4 [6: 2: 5: 2: 5:
2: 6] sts, (K1, K2tog, yfwd) 1 [1: 0: 1: 0: 1: 0: 1] times,
K1 [3: 2: 2: 2: 2: 2: 3].

**Row 11:** K2 [1: 1: 0: 1: 0: 1: 1], (yfwd, sl 1, K2tog,
psso, yfwd) 1 [0: 0: 0: 0: 0: 0: 0] times, (K2tog, yfwd)
0 [0: 1: 0: 1: 0: 1: 0] times, *K3, yfwd, sl 1, K2tog,
psso, yfwd, rep from * to last 2 [4: 6: 3: 6: 3: 6: 4] sts,
(K3, yfwd, sl 1, K1, psso) 0 [0: 1: 0: 1: 0: 1: 0] times,
K2 [4: 1: 3: 1: 3: 1: 4].

**Row 12:** Purl.

These 12 rows form patt.

Cont in patt, shaping side seams by inc 1 st at each end
of 5th and foll 16th row, taking inc sts into patt.
89 [93: 97: 103: 109: 115: 121: 129] sts.

Work 33 [33: 31: 39: 37: 43: 39: 45] rows, ending with
RS facing for next row. (Back should meas 25 [25: 24:
27: 26: 28: 27: 29] cm.)

**Shape armholes**

Keeping patt correct, cast off 3 [4: 4: 5: 5: 6: 6: 7] sts
at beg of next 2 rows.

83 [85: 89: 93: 99: 103: 109: 115] sts.

Dec 1 st at each end of next 3 [3: 5: 5: 7: 7: 9: 9] rows,
then on foll 4 [4: 3: 3: 3: 3: 2: 4] alt rows.

69 [71: 73: 77: 79: 83: 87: 89] sts.

Cont straight until armhole meas 18 [18: 19: 19: 20: 20:
21: 21] cm, ending with RS facing for next row.

**Shape shoulders and back neck**

**Next row (RS):** Cast off 5 [5: 6: 6: 6: 7: 8: 8] sts, patt
until there are 16 [17: 17: 19: 19: 20: 21: 22] sts on
right needle and turn, leaving rem sts on a holder.

Work each side of neck separately.

Cast off 3 sts at beg of next row, 5 [5: 6: 6: 6: 7: 8: 8] sts
at beg of foll row, then 3 sts at beg of next row.

Cast off rem 5 [6: 5: 7: 7: 7: 7: 8] sts.

With RS facing, rejoin yarn to rem sts, cast off centre
27 [27: 27: 27: 29: 29: 29: 29] sts, patt to end.

Complete to match first side, reversing shapings.

## LEFT FRONT

Using 3¾mm (US 5) needles cast on 40 [42: 44: 47: 50:
53: 56: 60] sts.

Work in g st for 12 rows, ending with RS facing for
next row.

Change to 4mm (US 6) needles.

**Row 1 (RS):** K1 [3: 1: 2: 1: 2: 1: 3], (K2tog, yfwd)
1 [1: 0: 1: 0: 1: 0: 1] times, *K1, yfwd, sl 1, K1,
psso, K1, K2tog, yfwd, rep from * to last st, K1.

**Row 2 and every foll alt row:** Purl.

**Rows 3 and 5**: As row 1.

**Row 7:** K0 [2: 1: 1: 1: 1: 1: 2], (K2tog, yfwd, K1) 1 [1:
0: 1: 0: 1: 0: 1] times, *K2, yfwd, sl 1, K2tog, psso,
yfwd, K1, rep from * to last st, K1.

**Row 9:** K1 [3: 1: 2: 1: 2: 1: 3], (yfwd, sl 1, K1, psso)
1 [1: 0: 1: 0: 1: 0: 1] times, *K1, K2tog, yfwd, K1,
yfwd, sl 1, K1, psso, rep from * to last st, K1.

**Row 11:** K2 [1: 1: 0: 1: 0: 1: 1], (yfwd, sl 1, K2tog,
psso, yfwd) 1 [0: 0: 0: 0: 0: 0: 0] times, (K2tog, yfwd)
0 [0: 1: 0: 1: 0: 1: 0] times, *K3, yfwd, sl 1, K2tog,
psso, yfwd, rep from * to last 5 sts, K3, yfwd, sl 1, K1,
psso.

**Row 12**: Purl.

These 12 rows form patt.

Cont in patt for a further 6 [6: 4: 12: 10: 16: 12: 18]
rows, shaping side seam by inc 1 [1: 0: 1: 1: 1: 1: 1] st
at beg of 5th of these rows, taking inc st into patt and
ending with RS facing for next row.

41 [43: 44: 48: 51: 54: 57: 61] sts.

**Shape front slope**

Keeping patt correct, dec 1 st at end of next and 2 [2:
0: 0: 2: 2: 0: 0] foll 4th rows, then on 6 [6: 7: 7: 6: 6: 7:
7] foll 6th rows **and at same time** inc 1 st at beg of
15th [15th: next: 9th: 11th: 5th: 9th: 3rd] and 0 [0: 1: 0:
0: 0: 0: 0] foll 16th row.

33 [35: 38: 41: 43: 46: 50: 54] sts.

Work 3 [3: 5: 5: 3: 3: 5: 5] rows, ending with RS facing
for next row.

**Shape armhole**

Keeping patt correct, cast off 3 [4: 4: 5: 5: 6: 6: 7] sts
at beg and dec 0 [0: 1: 1: 0: 0: 1: 1] st at end of next
row. 30 [31: 33: 35: 38: 40: 43: 46] sts.

Work 1 row.

Dec 1 st at armhole edge of next 3 [3: 5: 5: 7: 7: 9: 9]
rows, then on foll 4 [4: 3: 3: 3: 3: 2: 4] alt rows **and at
same time** dec 1 st at front slope edge of next [next:
5th: 5th: next: next: 5th: 5th] and every foll 6th row.

21 [22: 23: 25: 25: 27: 30: 30] sts.

Dec 1 st at front slope edge **only** on 2nd [2nd: 6th: 6th:
6th: 6th: 4th: 6th] and every foll 6th row until 15 [16:
17: 19: 19: 21: 23: 24] sts rem.

Cont straight until left front matches back to beg of
shoulder shaping, ending with RS facing for next row.

**Shape shoulder**

Cast off 5 [5: 6: 6: 6: 7: 8: 8] sts at beg of next and foll
alt row.

Work 1 row.
Cast off rem 5 [6: 5: 7: 7: 7: 7: 8] sts.

## RIGHT FRONT
Using 3¾mm (US 5) needles cast on 40 [42: 44: 47: 50: 53: 56: 60] sts.

Work in g st for 12 rows, ending with RS facing for next row.

Change to 4mm (US 6) needles.

**Row 1 (RS):** *K1, yfwd, sl 1, K1, psso, K1, K2tog, yfwd, rep from * to last 4 [6: 2: 5: 2: 5: 2: 6] sts, (K1, yfwd, sl 1, K1, psso) 1 [1: 0: 1: 0: 1: 0: 1] times, K1 [3: 2: 2: 2: 2: 2: 3].

**Row 2 and every foll alt row**: Purl.

**Rows 3 and 5**: As row 1.

**Row 7:** *K2, yfwd, sl 1, K2tog, psso, yfwd, K1, rep from * to last 4 [6: 2: 5: 2: 5: 2: 6] sts, (K2, yfwd, sl 1, K1, psso) 1 [1: 0: 1: 0: 1: 0: 1] times, K0 [2: 2: 1: 2: 1: 2: 2].

**Row 9:** *K1, K2tog, yfwd, K1, yfwd, sl 1, K1, psso, rep from * to last 4 [6: 2: 5: 2: 5: 2: 6] sts, (K1, K2tog, yfwd) 1 [1: 0: 1: 0: 1: 0: 1] times, K1 [3: 2: 2: 2: 2: 2: 3].

**Row 11:** K2tog, yfwd, *K3, yfwd, sl 1, K2tog, psso, yfwd, rep from * to last 2 [4: 6: 3: 6: 3: 6: 4] sts, (K3, yfwd, sl 1, K1, psso) 0 [0: 1: 0: 1: 0: 1: 0] times, K2 [4: 1: 3: 1: 3: 1: 4].

**Row 12**: Purl.

These 12 rows form patt.

Cont in patt for a further 6 [6: 4: 12: 10: 16: 12: 18] rows, shaping side seam by inc 1 [1: 0: 1: 1: 1: 1: 1] st at end of 5th of these rows, taking inc st into patt and ending with RS facing for next row.

41 [43: 44: 48: 51: 54: 57: 61] sts.

Complete to match left front, reversing shapings.

## SLEEVES
Using 3¾mm (US 5) needles cast on 51 [51: 53: 53: 55: 55: 57: 57] sts.

Work in g st for 12 rows, ending with RS facing for next row.

Change to 4mm (US 6) needles.

**Row 1 (RS):** K2 [2: 3: 3: 0: 0: 1: 1], (K2tog, yfwd) 1 [1: 1: 1: 0: 0: 0: 0] times, *K1, yfwd, sl 1, K1, psso, K1, K2tog, yfwd, rep from * to last 5 [5: 6: 6: 1: 1: 2: 2] sts, (K1, yfwd, sl 1, K1, psso) 1 [1: 1: 1: 0: 0: 0: 0] times, K2 [2: 3: 3: 1: 1: 2: 2].

**Row 2 and every foll alt row**: Purl.

**Row 3:** Inc in first st, K1 [1: 2: 2: 0: 0: 0: 0], (yfwd, sl 1, K1, psso, K1) 0 [0: 0: 0: 1: 1: 0: 0] times, (K2tog, yfwd) 1 [1: 1: 1: 1: 1: 1: 0] times, *K1, yfwd, sl 1, K1, psso, K1, K2tog, yfwd, rep from * to last 5 [5: 6: 6: 1: 1: 2: 2] sts, (K1, yfwd, sl 1, K1, psso) 1 [1: 1: 1: 0: 0: 0: 0] times, K1 [1: 2: 2: 0: 0: 1: 1], inc in last st.
53 [53: 55: 55: 57: 57: 59: 59] sts.

**Row 5:** K3 [3: 0: 0: 1: 1: 2: 2], (K2tog, yfwd) 1 [1: 0: 0: 0: 0: 0: 0] times, *K1, yfwd, sl 1, K1, psso, K1, K2tog, yfwd, rep from * to last 6 [6: 1: 1: 2: 2: 3: 3] sts, (K1, yfwd, sl 1, K1, psso) 1 [1: 0: 0: 0: 0: 0: 0] times, K3 [3: 1: 1: 2: 2: 3: 3].

**Row 7:** Inc in first st, K0 [0: 1: 1: 0: 0: 1: 1], (yfwd, sl 1, K2tog, psso, K1) 1 [1: 1: 1: 0: 0: 0: 0] times, *K2, yfwd, sl 1, K2tog, psso, yfwd, K1, rep from * to last 6 [6: 1: 1: 2: 2: 3: 3] sts, (K2, yfwd, sl 1, K2tog, psso, yfwd) 1 [1: 0: 0: 0: 0: 0: 0] times, K0 [0: 0: 0: 1: 1: 2: 2], inc in last st. 55 [55: 57: 57: 59: 59: 61: 61] sts.

**Row 9:** K0 [0: 1: 1: 2: 2: 1: 1], (yfwd, sl 1, K1, psso) 0 [0: 0: 0: 0: 1: 1] times, *K1, K2tog, yfwd, K1, yfwd, sl 1, K1, psso, rep from * to last 1 [1: 2: 2: 3: 3: 4: 4] sts, (K1, K2tog, yfwd) 0 [0: 0: 0: 0: 0: 1: 1] times, K1 [1: 2: 2: 3: 3: 1: 1].

**Row 11:** Inc in first st, K1 [1: 0: 0: 0: 0: 1: 1], (yfwd, sl 1, K2tog, psso, yfwd) 0 [0: 0: 0: 1: 1: 1: 1] times, (K2tog, yfwd) 0 [0: 1: 1: 0: 0: 0: 0] times, *K3, yfwd, sl 1, K2tog, psso, yfwd, rep from * to last 5 [5: 6: 6: 1: 1: 2: 2] sts, (K3, yfwd, sl 1, K1, psso) 0 [0: 1: 1: 0: 0: 0: 0] times, K4 [4: 0: 0: 0: 0: 1: 1], inc in last st. 57 [57: 59: 59: 61: 61: 63: 63] sts.

**Row 12:** Purl.

These 12 rows form patt and beg sleeve shaping.

Cont in patt, shaping sides by inc 1 st at each end of 3rd and every foll 4th row to 63 [69: 67: 73: 73: 79: 83: 89] sts, then on every foll 6th row until there are 81 [83: 85: 87: 89: 91: 93: 95] sts, taking inc sts into patt.

Cont straight until sleeve meas 34 [34: 35: 35: 36: 36: 35: 35] cm, ending with RS facing for next row.

**Shape top**
Keeping patt correct, cast off 3 [4: 4: 5: 5: 6: 6: 7] sts at beg of next 2 rows. 75 [75: 77: 77: 79: 79: 81: 81] sts.

Cast off 3 sts at beg of next 0 [0: 6: 6: 12: 12: 18: 18] rows, then 4 sts at beg of foll 12 [12: 8: 8: 4: 4: 0: 0] rows.

Cast off rem 27 sts.

## MAKING UP
Press as described on the information page.

Join both shoulder seams using back stitch, or mattress stitch if preferred.

**Front band**
With RS facing and using 3¾mm (US 5) circular needle, beg and ending at cast-on edges, pick up and knit 15 [15: 13: 19: 17: 21: 19: 23] sts up right front opening edge to beg of front slope shaping, 79 [79: 81: 81: 84: 84: 86: 86] sts up right front slope, 39 [39: 39: 39: 41: 41: 41: 41] sts from back, 79 [79: 81: 81: 84: 84: 86: 86] sts down left front slope to beg of front slope shaping, then 15 [15: 13: 19: 17: 21: 19: 23] sts down left front opening edge. 227 [227: 227: 239: 243: 251: 251: 259] sts.

Work in g st for 5 rows, ending with RS facing for next row.

**Row 6 (RS):** K3, cast off 2 sts (to make first buttonhole - cast on 2 sts over these cast off sts on next row), K until there are 7 [7: 5: 11: 9: 13: 11: 15] sts on right needle after cast-off, cast off 2 sts (to make second buttonhole - cast on 2 sts over these cast off sts on next row), K to end.

Work in g st for a further 6 rows, ending with **WS** facing for next row.

Cast off knitwise (on **WS**).

See information page for finishing instructions, setting in sleeves using the set-in method.

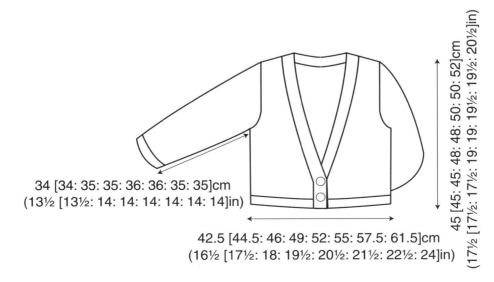

34 [34: 35: 35: 36: 36: 35: 35]cm
(13½ [13½: 14: 14: 14: 14: 14: 14]in)

42.5 [44.5: 46: 49: 52: 55: 57.5: 61.5]cm
(16½ [17½: 18: 19½: 20½: 21½: 22½: 24]in)

45 [45: 45: 48: 48: 50: 50: 52]cm
(17½ [17½: 17½: 19: 19: 19½: 19½: 20½]in)

# Thyme

main image page 12

### SIZE

|  | S | M | L | XL |  |
|---|---|---|---|---|---|
| To fit bust |  |  |  |  |  |
|  | 81-86 | 91-97 | 102-107 | 112-117 | cm |
|  | 32-34 | 36-38 | 40-42 | 44-46 | in |

### YARN

**Rowan Purleife Organic Wool DK**

|  | 11 | 12 | 12 | 13 | x 50gm |
|---|---|---|---|---|---|

(photographed in Horsetail 605)

### CROCHET HOOK

4.00mm (no 8) (US G6) crochet hook

### TENSION

23 sts and 8½ rows to 10 cm measured over patt using 4.00mm (US G6) hook.

### UK CROCHET ABBREVIATIONS

**ch** = chain; **dc** = double crochet; **ss** = slip stitch; **sp** = space; **tr** = treble; **tr2tog** = (yarn over hook and insert hook as indicated, yarn over hook and draw loop through, yarn over hook and draw through 2 loops) twice, yarn over hook and draw through all 3 loops on hook.

## BACK

Using 4.00mm (US G6) hook make 120 [129: 147: 156] ch.

**Row 1 (RS):** 1 dc into 2nd ch from hook, 1 dc into each ch to end, turn. 119 [128: 146: 155] sts.

**Row 2:** 1 ch (does NOT count as st), 1 dc into each dc to end, turn.

Rep last row until work meas 4 cm, ending with RS facing for next row.

**Next row (RS):** 3 ch (counts as first tr), miss dc at base of 3 ch, 1 tr into next dc, *miss 3 dc, (3 tr, 1 ch and 3 tr) into next dc, miss 3 dc, 1 tr into each of next 2 dc, rep from * to end, turn. 13 [14: 16: 17] patt reps.

Now work in patt as folls:

**Row 1:** 3 ch (counts as first tr), miss tr at base of 3 ch, 1 tr into next tr, *miss 2 tr, 1 tr into next tr, 1 ch, (1 tr, 1 ch and 1 tr) into next ch sp, 1 ch, 1 tr into next tr, miss 2 tr, 1 tr into each of next 2 tr, rep from * to end, working tr at end of last rep into top of 3 ch at beg of previous row, turn.

**Row 2:** 3 ch (counts as first tr), miss tr at base of 3 ch, 1 tr into next tr, *miss (1 tr, 1 ch and 1 tr), (2 tr, 3 ch and 2 tr) into next ch sp, miss (1 tr, 1 ch and 1 tr), 1 tr into each of next 2 tr, rep from * to end, working tr at end of last rep into top of 3 ch at beg of previous row, turn.

**Row 3:** 3 ch (counts as first tr), miss tr at base of 3 ch, 1 tr into next tr, *miss 2 tr, (3 tr, 1 ch and 3 tr) into next ch sp, miss 2 tr, 1 tr into each of next 2 tr, rep from * to end, working tr at end of last rep into top of 3 ch at beg of previous row, turn.

These 3 rows form patt.

Cont in patt, shaping side seams as folls:

**Row 4:** 3 ch (does NOT count as st), miss tr at base of 3 ch, 1 tr into next tr - 1 st decreased, patt to last 2 sts, tr2tog over last 2 sts - 1 st decreased, turn.

**Row 5:** 3 ch (counts as first tr), miss tr2tog at base of 3 ch, patt to last st, 1 tr into last tr, turn (leaving 3 ch at beg of previous row unworked).

**Row 6:** 3 ch (counts as first tr), miss 3 tr at end of previous row, (2 tr, 1 ch and 3 tr) into next ch sp, miss 2 tr, 1 tr into each of next 2 tr - 1 st decreased, patt until the "1 tr into each of next 2 tr" has been worked at end of last full patt rep, miss 2 tr, (3 tr, 1 ch and 2 tr) into next ch sp, miss 2 tr, 1 tr into top of 3 ch at beg of previous row - 1 st decreased, turn.

**Row 7:** 4 ch (counts as 1 tr and 1 ch), miss 3 tr at end of previous row, (1 tr, 1 ch and 1 tr) into next ch sp), 1 ch, 1 tr into next tr, miss 2 tr, 1 tr into each of next 2 tr, patt until the "1 tr into each of next 2 tr" has been worked at end of last full patt rep, miss 2 tr, 1 tr into next tr, 1 ch, (1 tr, 1 ch and 1 tr) into next ch sp, 1 ch, miss 2 tr, 1 tr into top of 3 ch at beg of previous row, turn.

**Row 8:** 3 ch (counts as first tr), miss (1 tr, 1 ch and 1 tr) at end of previous row, (1 tr, 3 ch and 2 tr) into next ch sp, miss (1 tr, 1 ch and 1 tr), 1 tr into each of next 2 tr - 1 st decreased, patt until the "1 tr into each of next 2 tr" has been worked at end of last full patt rep, miss (1 tr, 1 ch and 1 tr), (2 tr, 3 ch and 1 tr) into next ch sp, miss (1 tr and 1 ch), 1 tr into 3rd of 4 ch at beg of previous row - 1 st decreased, turn.

**Row 9:** 3 ch (counts as first tr), miss 2 tr at end of previous row, (1 tr, 1 ch and 3 tr) into next ch sp, miss 2 tr, 1 tr into each of next 2 tr, patt until the "1 tr into each of next 2 tr" has been worked at end of last full patt rep, miss 2 tr, (3 tr, 1 ch and 1 tr) into next ch sp, miss 1 tr, 1 tr into top of 3 ch at beg of previous row, turn.

**Row 10:** 4 ch (counts as 1 tr and 1 ch), miss 2 tr at end of previous row, 1 tr into next ch sp, 1 ch, 1 tr into next tr, miss 2 tr, 1 tr into each of next 2 tr - 1 st decreased, patt until the "1 tr into each of next 2 tr" has been worked at end of last full patt rep, miss 2 tr, 1 tr into next tr, 1 ch, 1 tr into next ch sp, 1 ch, miss 1 tr, 1 tr into top of 3 ch at beg of previous row - 1 st decreased, turn.

**Row 11:** 5 ch (counts as 1 tr and 2 ch), miss tr at end of previous row, 2 tr into next ch sp, miss (1 tr, 1 ch and 1 tr), 1 tr into each of next 2 tr, patt until the "1 tr into each of next 2 tr" has been worked at end of last full patt rep, miss (1 tr, 1 ch and 1 tr), 2 tr into next ch sp, 2 ch, 1 tr into 3rd of 4 ch at beg of previous row, turn.

**Row 12:** 3 ch (counts as first tr), miss tr at end of previous row, 3 tr into next ch sp, miss 2 tr, 1 tr into each of next 2 tr - 1 st decreased, patt until the "1 tr into each of next 2 tr" has been worked at end of last full patt rep, miss 2 tr, 3 tr into next ch sp, 1 tr into 3rd of 5 ch at beg of previous row - 1 st decreased, turn.

**Row 13:** 3 ch (counts as first tr), 1 tr into tr at base of 3 ch, 1 ch, 1 tr into next tr, miss 2 tr, 1 tr into each of next 2 tr, patt until the "1 tr into each of next 2 tr" has been worked at end of last full patt rep, miss 2 tr, 1 tr into next tr, 1 ch, 2 tr into top of 3 ch at beg of previous row, turn.

**Row 14:** 3 ch (counts as first tr), 2 tr into tr at base of 3 ch, miss (1 tr, 1 ch and 1 tr), 1 tr into each of next 2 tr - 1 st decreased, patt until the "1 tr into each of next 2 tr" has been worked at end of last full patt rep, miss (1 tr, 1 ch and 1 tr), 3 tr into top of 3 ch at beg of previous row - 1 st decreased, turn.

**Row 15:** 3 ch (counts as first tr), 2 tr into tr at base of 3 ch, miss 2 tr, 1 tr into each of next 2 tr, patt until the "1 tr into each of next 2 tr" has been worked at end of last full patt rep, miss 2 tr, 3 tr into top of 3 ch at beg of previous row, turn.

**Row 16:** 3 ch (counts as first tr), 1 tr into tr at base of 3 ch, miss 2 tr, 1 tr into each of next 2 tr - 1 st decreased, patt until the "1 tr into each of next 2 tr" has been worked at end of last full patt rep, miss 2 tr, 2 tr into top of 3 ch at beg of previous row - 1 st decreased, turn.

**Row 17:** 3 ch (counts as first tr), miss tr at base of 3 ch, 1 tr into each of next 3 tr, patt until the "1 tr into each of next 2 tr" has been worked at end of last full patt rep,

1 tr into next tr, 1 tr into top of 3 ch at beg of previous row, turn.

**Row 18:** 3 ch (counts as first tr), miss tr at base of 3 ch and next tr, 1 tr into each of next 2 tr - 1 st decreased, patt until the "1 tr into each of next 2 tr" has been worked at end of last full patt rep, miss 1 tr, 1 tr into top of 3 ch at beg of previous row - 1 st decreased, turn.

**Row 19:** 3 ch (counts as first tr), miss tr at base of 3 ch, 1 tr into each of next 2 tr, patt until the "1 tr into each of next 2 tr" has been worked at end of last full patt rep, 1 tr into top of 3 ch at beg of previous row, turn.

**Row 20:** 3 ch (counts as first tr), miss tr at base of 3 ch and next tr, 1 tr into next tr - 1 st decreased, patt until **before** the "1 tr into each of next 2 tr" is to be worked at end of last full patt rep, 1 tr into first of these 2 tr, miss next tr, 1 tr into top of 3 ch at beg of previous row - 1 st decreased, turn. 101 [110: 128: 137] sts, 11 [12: 14: 15] patt reps.

Cont straight until back meas 40 [41: 42: 43] cm.

**Shape armholes**

**Next row:** ss across and into 10th st, 3 ch (counts as first tr), miss st at base of 3 ch - 9 sts decreased, 1 tr into next tr, patt to last 9 sts and turn, leaving rem sts unworked - 9 sts decreased. 83 [92: 110: 119] sts, 9 [10: 12: 13] patt reps.

Working all armhole decreases in same way as side seam decreases, dec 1 st at each end of next 1 [3: 9: 10] rows. 81 [86: 92: 99] sts. (**Note:** side seam decreases were worked on every **alt** row - here they are to be worked on **every** row.)

Cont straight until armhole meas 18 [19: 20: 21] cm.

**Shape shoulders and back neck**

**Next row:** Patt 20 [22: 24: 27] sts and turn, leaving rem sts unworked.

Work each side of neck separately.

Dec 1 st at neck edge of next row. 19 [21: 23: 26] sts.
Fasten off.

Return to last complete row worked, miss centre 41 [42: 44: 45] sts, rejoin yarn to next st, patt to end.

Complete to match first side, reversing shapings.

## FRONT

Work as given for back until 7 [7: 8: 8] rows less have

been worked than on back to shoulder fasten-off.

**Shape neck**

**Next row:** Patt 25 [27: 30: 33] sts and turn, leaving rem sts unworked.

Work each side of neck separately.

Working all neck decreases in same way as side seam decreases, dec 1 st at neck edge of next 6 [6: 7: 7] rows. 19 [21: 23: 26] sts.

**Shape shoulder**

Fasten off.

Return to last complete row worked, miss centre 31 [32: 32: 33] sts, rejoin yarn to next st, patt to end.

Complete to match first side, reversing shapings.

## SLEEVES

Using 4.00mm (US G6) hook make 57 [57: 66: 66] ch.

**Row 1 (RS):** 1 dc into 2nd ch from hook, 1 dc into each ch to end, turn. 56 [56: 65: 65] sts.

**Row 2:** 1 ch (does NOT count as st), 1 dc into each dc to end, turn.

Rep last row until work meas 4 cm, ending with RS facing for next row.

**Next row (RS):** 3 ch (counts as first tr), miss dc at base of 3 ch, 1 tr into next dc, *miss 3 dc, (3 tr, 1 ch and 3 tr) into next dc, miss 3 dc, 1 tr into each of next 2 dc, rep from * to end, turn. 6 [6: 7: 7] patt reps.

Now work in patt as folls:

**Row 1:** 3 ch (counts as first tr), miss tr at base of 3 ch, 1 tr into next tr, *miss 2 tr, 1 tr into next tr, 1 ch, (1 tr, 1 ch and 1 tr) into next ch sp, 1 ch, 1 tr into next tr, miss 2 tr, 1 tr into each of next 2 tr, rep from * to end, working tr at end of last rep into top of 3 ch at beg of previous row, turn.

This row sets position of patt as given for back.

Cont in patt, shaping sides as folls:

**Row 2:** 3 ch (counts as first tr), 1 tr into tr at base of 3 ch - 1 st increased, 1 tr into next tr, patt until the "1 tr into each of next 2 tr" has been worked at end of last full patt rep (2nd of these tr is worked into top of 3 ch at beg of previous row), 1 tr into same place as last tr - 1 st increased, turn.

**Row 3:** 3 ch (counts as first tr), 1 tr into tr at base of 3 ch

- 1 st increased, 1 tr into each of next 2 tr, patt until the "1 tr into each of next 2 tr" has been worked at end of last full patt rep, 2 tr into top of 3 ch at beg of previous row - 1 st increased, turn.

**Row 4:** 3 ch (counts as first tr), miss tr at base of 3 ch, 1 tr into each of next 3 tr, patt until the "1 tr into each of next 2 tr" has been worked at end of last full patt rep, 1 tr into next tr, 1 tr into top of 3 ch at beg of previous row, turn.

Working all increased sts as trs (as set by last 3 rows) until there are sufficient to work in patt, cont as folls:
Inc 1 st at each end of next 2 rows.
Work 1 row.
Rep last 3 rows 7 [7: 6: 6] times more. 92 [92: 97: 97] sts.
Work 0 [1: 0: 1] row, inc 1 st at each end of this row. 92 [94: 97: 99] sts.
Cont straight until sleeve meas 44 [45: 46: 46] cm.

**Shape top**

Working all shaping in same way as for armholes and front neck, dec 9 sts at each end of next row.
74 [76: 79: 81] sts.

Dec 1 st at each end of next 7 [8: 9: 10] rows.
60 [60: 61: 61] sts.
Fasten off.

## MAKING UP

Press as described on the information page.
Join both shoulder seams using back stitch, or mattress stitch if preferred.

**Neckband and ties**

With RS facing and using 4.00mm (US G6) hook, make 57 ch (for first tie), 1 dc into centre front neck point, then work 1 round of dc evenly around entire neck edge to centre front neck, turn.

**Next row (WS):** 58 ch (for second tie), 1 dc into 2nd ch from hook, 1 dc into each of next 56 ch, 1 dc into each dc and ch to end, turn.

**Next row:** 1 ch (does NOT count as st), 1 dc into each dc to end, turn.

Rep last row once more.
Fasten off.
See information page for finishing instructions, setting in sleeves using the set-in method.

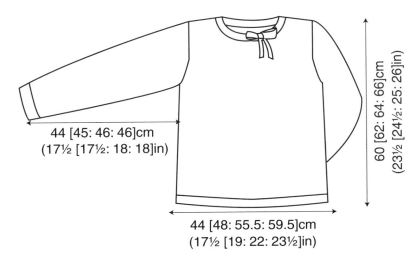

44 [45: 46: 46]cm
(17½ [17½: 18: 18]in)

60 [62: 64: 66]cm
(23½ [24½: 25: 26]in)

44 [48: 55.5: 59.5]cm
(17½ [19: 22: 23½]in)

# Melissa

main image page 19

## SIZE

| 8 | 10 | 12 | 14 | 16 | 18 | 20 | 22 | |
|---|----|----|----|----|----|----|----|---|
| To fit bust | | | | | | | | |
| 81 | 86 | 91 | 97 | 102 | 107 | 112 | 117 | cm |
| 32 | 34 | 36 | 38 | 40 | 42 | 44 | 46 | in |

## YARN

**Rowan Purelife Organic Wool DK**

| A Aran White | 600 | | | | | | | |
|---|---|---|---|---|---|---|---|---|
| 8 | 8 | 8 | 9 | 10 | 10 | 10 | 11 | x 50gm |
| B Horsetail | 605 | | | | | | | |
| 1 | 1 | 1 | 1 | 1 | 1 | 1 | 1 | x 50gm |

## NEEDLES

1 pair 3¾mm (no 9) (US 5) needles
1 pair 4mm (no 8) (US 6) needles

## TENSION

22 sts and 30 rows to 10 cm measured over st st using 4mm (US 6) needles.

## BACK

Using 3¾mm (US 5) needles and yarn A cast on 93 [97: 101: 107: 115: 121: 127: 135] sts.
Work in g st for 2 rows, ending with RS facing for next row.
Change to 4mm (US 6) needles.
Beg with a K row, work in st st until back meas 34 [34: 33: 36: 35: 37: 36: 38] cm, ending with RS facing for next row.

### Shape armholes

Cast off 3 [4: 4: 5: 5: 6: 6: 7] sts at beg of next 2 rows.
87 [89: 93: 97: 105: 109: 115: 121] sts.
Dec 1 st at each end of next 3 [3: 5: 5: 7: 7: 9: 9] rows, then on foll 4 [4: 3: 3: 4: 4: 3: 5] alt rows.
73 [75: 77: 81: 83: 87: 91: 93] sts.
Cont straight until armhole meas 18 [18: 19: 19: 20: 20: 21: 21] cm, ending with RS facing for next row.

### Shape shoulders and back neck

**Next row (RS):** Cast off 6 [6: 7: 7: 7: 8: 9: 9] sts, K until there are 18 [19: 19: 21: 21: 22: 23: 24] sts on right needle and turn, leaving rem sts on a holder.
Work each side of neck separately.
Cast off 3 sts at beg of next row, 6 [6: 7: 7: 7: 8: 9: 9] sts at beg of foll row, then 3 sts at beg of next row.
Cast off rem 6 [7: 6: 8: 8: 8: 8: 9] sts.
With RS facing, rejoin yarn to rem sts, cast off centre 25 [25: 25: 25: 27: 27: 27: 27] sts, K to end.
Complete to match first side, reversing shapings.

## FRONT

Work as given for back until 22 [22: 22: 24: 24: 24: 26: 26] rows less have been worked than on back to beg of shoulder shaping, ending with RS facing for next row.

### Shape neck

**Next row (RS):** K28 [29: 30: 33: 33: 35: 38: 39] and turn, leaving rem sts on a holder.
Work each side of neck separately.
Dec 1 st at neck edge of next 6 rows, then on foll 2 [2:

2: 3: 3: 3: 3: 4: 4] alt rows, then on 2 foll 4th rows.
18 [19: 20: 22: 22: 24: 26: 27] sts.
Work 3 rows, ending with RS facing for next row.

### Shape shoulder

Cast off 6 [6: 7: 7: 7: 8: 9: 9] sts at beg of next and foll alt row.
Work 1 row.
Cast off rem 6 [7: 6: 8: 8: 8: 8: 9] sts.
With RS facing, rejoin yarn to rem sts, cast off centre 17 [17: 17: 15: 17: 17: 15: 15] sts, K to end.
Complete to match first side, reversing shapings.

## SLEEVES

Using 3¾mm (US 5) needles and yarn A cast on 49 [49: 51: 51: 53: 53: 55: 55] sts.
Work in g st for 2 rows, ending with RS facing for next row.

Change to 4mm (US 6) needles.
Beg with a K row, work in st st, inc 1 st at each end of 5th [5th: 5th: 5th: 5th: 3rd: 3rd: 3rd] and every foll 6th [6th: 6th: 6th: 6th: 6th: 4th: 4th] row to 75 [83: 83: 91: 89: 95: 61: 67] sts, then on every foll 8th [8th: 8th: -: 8th: -: 6th: 6th] row until there are 85 [87: 89: -: 93: -: 97: 99] sts.
Cont straight until sleeve meas 44 [44: 45: 45: 46: 46: 45: 45] cm, ending with RS facing for next row.

### Shape top

Cast off 3 [4: 4: 5: 5: 6: 6: 7] sts at beg of next 2 rows.
79 [79: 81: 81: 83: 83: 85: 85] sts.
Dec 1 st at each end of next 5 rows, then on every foll alt row to 63 sts, then on foll 15 rows, ending with RS facing for next row. 33 sts.
Cast off 5 sts at beg of next 2 rows.
Cast off rem 23 sts.

44 [44: 45: 45: 46: 46: 45: 45]cm
(17½ [17½: 17½: 17½:18: 18: 17½ : 17½]in)

54 [54: 54: 57: 57: 59: 59: 61]cm
(21½ [21½: 21½: 22½: 22½: 23: 23: 24]in)

42.5 [44: 46: 48.5: 52.5: 55: 57.5: 61.5]cm
(16½ [17½: 18: 19: 20½: 21½: 22½: 24]in)

## MAKING UP

Press as described on the information page.

Join right shoulder seam using back stitch, or mattress stitch if preferred.

**Neckband**

With RS facing, using 3¾mm (US 5) needles and yarn A, pick up and knit 22 [22: 22: 24: 24: 24: 26: 26] sts down left side of neck, 17 [17: 17: 15: 17: 17: 15: 15] sts from front, 22 [22: 22: 24: 24: 24: 26: 26] sts up right side of neck, then 37 [37: 37: 37: 39: 39: 39: 39] sts from back. 98 [98: 98: 100: 104: 104: 106: 106] sts.

Work in g st for 2 rows, ending with **WS** facing for next row.

Cast off knitwise (on **WS**).

See information page for finishing instructions, setting in sleeves using the set-in method.

Using yarn B and following diagram, embroider design onto front and sleeves using chain stitch.

Embroidery Diagram    photocopy at 200% for accurate size

Neckband

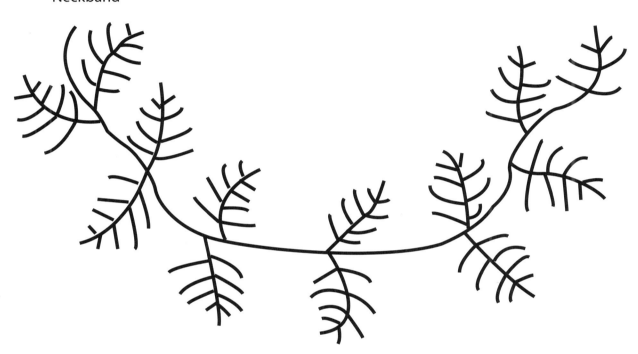

Sleeve.

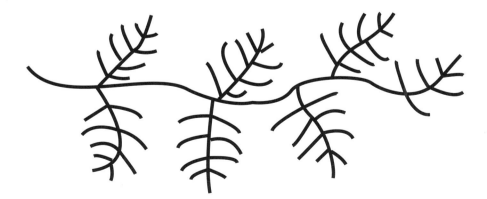

# information page

## Tension
Obtaining the correct tension is perhaps the single factor which can make the difference between a successful garment and a disastrous one. It controls both the shape and size of an article, so any variation, however slight, can distort the finished garment. Different designers feature in our books and it is their tension, given at the start of each pattern, which you must match. We recommend that you knit a square in pattern and/or stocking stitch (depending on the pattern instructions) of perhaps 5 – 10 more stitches and 5 – 10 more rows than those given in the tension note. Mark out the central 10cm square with pins. If you have too many stitches to 10cm try again using thicker needles, if you have too few stitches to 10cm try again using finer needles. Once you have achieved the correct tension your garment will be knitted to the measurements indicated in the size diagram shown at the end of the pattern.

## Sizing and Size Diagram Note
The instructions are given for the smallest size. Where they vary, work the figures in brackets for the larger sizes. One set of figures refers to all sizes. Included with most patterns in this brochure is a 'size diagram', or sketch of the finished garment and its dimensions. To help you choose the size of garment to knit please refer to the new sizing guide on page 34.

## Chart Note
Many of the patterns in the book are worked from charts. Each square on a chart represents a stitch and each line of squares a row of knitting. Each colour used is given a different letter and these are shown in the materials section, or in the key alongside the chart of each pattern.
When working from the charts, read odd rows (K) from right to left and even rows (P) from left to right, unless otherwise stated.

## Finishing Instructions
After working for hours knitting a garment, it seems a great pity that many garments are spoiled because such little care is taken in the pressing and finishing process. Follow the following tips for a truly professional looking garment.

## Pressing
Block out each piece of knitting and following the instructions on the ball band press the garment pieces, omitting the ribs.

## Tip
Take special care to press the edges, as this will make sewing up both easier and neater. If the ball band indicates that the fabric is not to be pressed, then covering the blocked out fabric with a damp white cotton cloth and leaving it to stand will have the desired effect. Darn in all ends neatly along the selvage edge or a colour join, as appropriate.

## Stitching
When stitching the pieces together, remember to match areas of colour and texture very carefully where they meet. Use a seam stitch such as back stitch or mattress stitch for all main knitting seams and join all ribs and neckband with mattress stitch, unless otherwise stated.

## Construction
Having completed the pattern instructions, join left shoulder and neckband seams as detailed above. Sew the top of the sleeve to the body of the garment using the method detailed in the pattern, referring to the appropriate guide:

## Straight cast-off sleeves
Place centre of cast-off edge of sleeve to shoulder seam. Sew top of sleeve to body, using markers as guidelines where applicable.

## Square set-in sleeves
Place centre of cast-off edge of sleeve to shoulder seam. Set sleeve head into armhole, the straight sides at top of sleeve to form a neat rightangle to cast-off sts at armhole on back and front.

## Shallow set-in sleeves
Place centre of cast off edge of sleeve to shoulder seam. Match decreases at beg of armhole shaping to decreases at top of sleeve. Sew sleeve head into armhole, easing in shapings.

## Set-in sleeves
Place centre of cast-off edge of sleeve to shoulder seam. Set in sleeve, easing sleeve head into armhole.

Join side and sleeve seams.
Slip stitch pocket edgings and linings into place.
Sew on buttons to correspond with buttonholes.
Ribbed welts and neckbands and any areas of garter stitch should not be pressed.

## Working a Lace Pattern
When working a lace pattern it is important to remember that if you are unable to work both the increase and corresponding decrease and vica versa, the stitches should be worked in stocking stitch.

# abbreviations

| | | | | | | |
|---|---|---|---|---|---|---|
| **K** | knit | **WS** | wrong side | | | |
| **P** | purl | **sl 1** | slip one stitch | | | |
| **st(s)** | stitch(es) | **psso** | pass slipped stitch over | | | |
| **inc** | increas(e)(ing) | **p2sso** | pass 2 slipped stitches over | | | |
| **dec** | decreas(e)(ing) | **tbl** | through back of loop | | | |
| **st st** | stocking stitch (1 row K, 1 row P) | **M1** | make one stitch by picking up | | | |
| **g st** | garter stitch (K every row) | | horizontal loop before next stitch and | | | |
| **beg** | begin(ning) | | knitting into back of it | | | |
| **foll** | following | **M1P** | make one stitch by picking up | | | |
| **rem** | remain(ing) | | horizontal loop before next stitch | | | |
| **rev st st** | reverse stocking stitch (1 row K, 1row P) | | and purling into back of it | | | |
| **rep** | repeat | **yfwd** | yarn forward | | | |
| **alt** | alternate | **yrn** | yarn round needle | | | |
| **cont** | continue | **meas** | measures | | | |
| **patt** | pattern | **0** | no stitches, times or rows | | | |
| **tog** | together | **-** | no stitches, times or rows for that size | | | |
| **mm** | millimetres | **yon** | yarn over needle | | | |
| **cm** | centimetres | **yfrn** | yarn forward round needle | | | |
| **in(s)** | inch(es) | **wyib** | with yarn at back | | | |
| **RS** | right side | | | | | |

**Crochet Terms**

UK crochet terms and abbreviations have been used throughout. The list below gives the US equivalent where they vary.

| ABBREV. | UK | US |
|---|---|---|
| **dc** | double crochet | single crochet |
| **htr** | half treble | half double crochet |
| **tr** | treble | double crochet |
| **dtr** | double treble | treble |
| **ttr** | triple treble | double treble |
| **qtr** | quadruple treble | triple treble |

# Experience Ratings

 Easy, straight forward knitting

Suitable for the average knitter

# Stockists

**AUSTRALIA**
Australian Country Spinners, 314 Albert Street, Brunswick, Victoria 3056.
*Tel:* (61) 3 9380 3888  *Fax:* (61) 3 9387 2674
*Email:* sales@auspinners.com.au

**AUSTRIA**
Coats Harlander GmbH, Autokaderstrasse 31, A -1210 Wien.
*Tel:* (01) 27716 – 0  *Fax:* (01) 27716 - 228

**BELGIUM**
Coats Benelux, Ring Oost 14A, Ninove, 9400, Belgium
*Tel:* 0346 35 37 00
*Email:* sales.coatsninove@coats.com

**CANADA**
Westminster Fibers Inc, 165 Ledge St, Nashua, NH03060
*Tel:* (1 603) 886 5041 / 5043
*Fax:* (1 603) 886 1056
*Email:* rowan@westminsterfibers.com

**CHINA**
Coats Shanghai Ltd, No 9 Building, Baosheng Road, Songjiang Industrial Zone, Shanghai.
*Tel:* (86- 21) 5774 3733
*Fax:* (86-21) 5774 3768

**DENMARK**
Coats Danmark A/S, Nannasgade 28, 2200 Kobenhavn N
*Tel:* (45) 35 86 90 50  *Fax:* ( 45) 35 82 15 10
*Email:* info@hpgruppen.dk
*Web:* www.hpgruppen.dk

**FINLAND**
Coats Opti Oy, Ketjutie 3, 04220 Kerava
*Tel:* (358) 9 274 871  *Fax:* (358) 9 2748 7330
*Email:* coatsopti.sales@coats.com

**FRANCE**
Coats France / Steiner Frères, SAS 100, avenue du Général de Gaulle, 18 500 Mehun-Sur-Yèvre
*Tel:* (33) 02 48 23 12 30  *Fax:* (33) 02 48 23 12 40

**GERMANY**
Coats GMbH, Kaiserstrasse 1, D-79341 Kenzingen
*Tel:* (49) 7644 8020  *Fax:* (49) 7644 802399
*Web:* www.coatsgmbh.de

**HOLLAND**
Coats Benelux, Ring Oost 14A, Ninove, 9400, Belgium
*Tel:* 0346 35 37 00
*Email:* sales.coatsninove@coats.com

**HONG KONG**
Coats China Holdings Ltd, 19/F Millennium City 2, 378 Kwun Tong Road, Kwun Tong, Kowloon
*Tel:* (852) 2798 6886  *Fax:* (852) 2305 0311

**ICELAND**
Storkurinn, Laugavegi 59, 101 Reykjavik
*Tel:* (354) 551 8258
*Email:* storkurinn@simnet.is

**ITALY**
Coats Cucirini s.r.l., Via Sarca 223, 20126 Milano
*Tel:* 800 992377  *Fax:* 0266111701
*Email:* servizio.clienti@coats.com

**JAPAN**
Puppy-Jardin Co Ltd, 3-8-11 Kudanminami Chiyodaku, Hiei Kudan Bldg. 5F, Tokyo
*Tel:* (81) 3 3222-7076  *Fax:* (81) 3 3222- 7066
*Email:* info@rowan-jaeger.com

**KOREA**
Coats Korea Co Ltd, 5F Kuckdong B/D, 935-40 Bangbae- Dong, Seocho-Gu, Seoul
*Tel:* (82) 2 521 6262.  *Fax:* (82) 2 521 5181

**LEBANON**
y.knot, Saifi Village, Mkhalissiya Street 162, Beirut,
*Tel:* (961) 1 992211  *Fax:* (961) 1 315553
*Email:* y.knot@cyberia.net.lb

**LUXEMBOURG**
Coats Benelux, Ring Oost 14A, Ninove, 9400, Belgium
*Tel:* 054 318989
*Email:* sales.coatsninove@coats.com

**MEXICO**
Estambres Crochet SA de CV, Aaron Saenz 1891-7, Monterrey, NL 64650 Mexico
*Tel:* +52 (81) 8335-3870

**NEW ZEALAND**
ACS New Zealand, 1 March Place, Belfast, Christchurch
*Tel:* 64-3-323-6665 *Fax:* 64-3-323-6660

**NORWAY**
Coats Knappehuset AS, Pb 100 Ulset, 5873 Bergen
*Tel:* (47) 55 53 93 00  *Fax:* (47) 55 53 93 93

**SINGAPORE**
Golden Dragon Store, 101 Upper Cross Street #02-51, People's Park Centre, Singapore 058357
*Tel:* (65) 6 5358454  *Fax:* (65) 6 2216278
*Email:* gdscraft@hotmail.com

**SOUTH AFRICA**
Arthur Bales PTY, PO Box 44644, Linden 2104
*Tel:* (27) 11 888 2401  *Fax:* (27) 11 782 6137

**SPAIN**
Oyambre, Pau Claris 145, 80009 Barcelona.
*Tel:* (34) 670 011957  *Fax:* (34) 93 4872672
*Email:* oyambre@oyambreonline.com

Coats Fabra, Santa Adria, Barcelona
*Tel:* 932908400  *Fax:* 932908409
*Email:* atencion.clientes@coats.com

**SWEDEN**
Coats Expotex AB, Division Craft, Box 297, 401 24 Goteborg
*Tel:* (46) 33 720 79 00  *Fax:* 46 31 47 16 50

**SWITZERLAND**
Coats Stroppel AG, Stroppelstr.16 CH -5300 Turgi (AG)
*Tel:* (41) 562981220  *Fax:* (41) 56 298 12 50

**TAIWAN**
Cactus Quality Co Ltd, P.O.Box 30 485, Taipei, Taiwan, R.O.C., Office: 7FL-2, No 140, Roosevelt Road, Sec 2,Taipei, Taiwan, R.O.C.
*Tel:* 886-2-23656527 *Fax:* 886-2-23656503
*Email:* cqcl@m17.hinet.net

**THAILAND**
Global Wide Trading, 10 Lad Prao Soi 88, Bangkok 10310
*Tel:* 00 662 933 9019 *Fax:* 00 662 933 9110
*Email:* theneedleworld@yahoo.com

**U.S.A.**
Westminster Fibers Inc, 165 Ledge St, Nashua, NH03060
*Tel:* (1 603) 886 5041 / 5043
*Fax:* (1 603) 886 1056
*Email:* rowan@westminsterfibers.com

**U.K**
Rowan, Green Lane Mill, Holmfirth, West Yorkshire, England HD9 2DX
*Tel:* +44 (0) 1484 681881
*Fax:* +44 (0) 1484 687920
*Email:* mail@knitrowan.com
*Web:* www.knitrowan.com

# Notes

# Notes

# Notes

**Photographer:** Moy Williams
**Styling:** Marie Wallin assisted by Sarah Hatton
**Art Direction:** Marie Wallin
**Hair and Make-up:** Francis Prescott
**Design Layout:** Lisa Richardson
**Models:** Rachel Blais - Premier Model Management
**Location:** Whitbysteads Farm, Askham, Penrith, Cumbria, CA10 2PG - Compass Locations
**With many thanks:** Tom & Victoria Lowther for their kind hospitality

**With special thanks to the following handknitters:**

Ann Banks, Joan Broadbent, Joyce Coop, Susan Grimes, Elizabeth Jones, Audrey Kidd, Joyce Sledmore, Elsie Eland, Ella Taylor,
Sandra Richardson, Pat Garden

First published in Great Britain in 2008 by Rowan Yarns Ltd, Green Lane Mill, Holmfirth, West Yorkshire, England, HD9 2DX
·Internet: www.knitrowan.com
© Copyright Rowan 2008
British Library Cataloguing in Publication Data Rowan Yarns – Rowan Purelife The Organic Wool Collection
ISBN 978-1-906007-47-8